How to Understand and Survive the Coming Tax Reforms

Donald B. Susswein

AMA Management Briefing

AMA MEMBERSHIP PUBLICATIONS DIVISION
AMERICAN MANAGEMENT ASSOCIATION

Y0-BVQ-830

Library of Congress Cataloging in Publication Data

Susswein, Donald B., 1953-
  How to understand and survive the coming tax reforms.

  (AMA management briefing)
  1. Taxation—Law and legislation—United States.
I. Title. II. Series.
KF6289.S87   1985   343.7304   85-1442
ISBN 0-8144-2315-9   347.3034

© 1985 Donald B. Susswein

First printing

Acknowledgments

There are many people whose assistance was critical to the success of this project.

George Mundstock, formerly of the Treasury Department's Office of Tax Policy and now of the University of Miami School of Law, provided insightful criticism of the manuscript, and made many useful suggestions. Elise Paylan, Catherine Porter, Sam Richardson, and Lorraine Jani gave valuable editorial comments and invaluable encouragement. Beverly and Philip Susswein helped guide me through the seeming maze of the publishing world, while Mitchell Radin helped with the seamless web of legalities involved in a project of this nature. Mary O'Meara performed a variety of critical secretarial tasks quickly, cheerfully, and well, and Joni Sarles did an excellent job reviewing technical data.

My colleagues and co-workers at the Senate Finance Committee, and at the House Ways and Means Committee, Joint Committee on Taxation, Treasury Department, and the other offices involved in the tax-writing process taught me a great deal and helped make Capitol Hill an exciting and congenial place to work.

My parents, Leonore and Arthur Susswein, are acknowledged last only because it is easier to say that they seem to have done all of the above, and more.

Acknowledgments

Contents

Contents

Foreword

Conservatism, Compassion, and the Cost of Governing

Senator Robert J. Dole (R., Kansas)
Majority Leader, United States Senate

"The tax laws are changing too fast." It's a complaint I heard often as Chairman of the Senate Finance Committee. "Even if the tax system is becoming more fair," the businessmen and tax professionals told me, "three major tax bills in four years were too much for anyone—even the IRS—to swallow." Maybe they're right.

I tried to explain the problems we were dealing with—not just meeting a bottom line of collecting a given amount of revenue—but reconciling deeply held attitudes about the tax system, the role of government in the economy, fairness, and the hundred other factors that Congress considers every time it "reopens the patient" to do surgery on the Internal Revenue Code.

This book does an excellent job of conveying just how difficult it is to weigh and balance the competing concerns involved in even the simplest piece of tax legislation. And of course, what the Treasury Department and others have put on the agenda in the name of "tax reform" is hardly simple. While I do not necessarily share all of the views expressed in this book, I must say that the author has flagged the critical issues for debate.

Deficit Reduction: The First Priority

In my view, the first priority for the 99th Congress should not be tax changes, but deficit reduction through spending restraint and reform of spending programs in all areas of government. When budget deficits are as serious a problem as they are today, spending reductions, not tax increases, are the key to a long-lasting solution.

A few years ago, the Capitol Hill budget battles made good copy for news stories: "Boll Weevils," "Gypsy Moths," and other creatures became metaphors for various political factions in the Congress. Now it's becoming fashionable for some to try to metamorphose into a new, more popular political animal: the Compassionate Fiscal Conservative. I suppose I've always thought of myself that way, long before these buzzwords began to enter common political parlance. But now, as the terms "compassion" and "conservatism" stand on the verge of becoming political clichés, I'd like to take a shot at redeeming them as meaningful political concepts.

Conservatism and the Economy

Conservatism, to me, is essentially a form of skepticism about government. Skepticism or distrust of government is, of course, the reason we have a Constitution and a Bill of Rights limiting the power of our national and state governments.

When it comes to economic policy, that skepticism is reflected in the view that government ought to intervene in the economic life of the nation *only* when there is a very strong case made for doing so. It's not that there is anything inherently evil, corrupt, or wasteful about government spending or regulation. It's just a belief, or prejudice, if you will, that tends to trust the wisdom of millions of individual economic decisions in the market, more than the wisdom of the Congress, in matters of economics.

The fascinating thing about the Treasury Department's tax reform proposal, whether you personally like it or not, is its remarkable intellectual consistency in insisting that the tax code should not be used to intervene in the economy. Of course, almost no one is willing to rule out government involvement in the economy, so the battle tends to be joined on the issue of whether a sufficient case for intervention has been made in any particular instance. There are those of us who look to intervention by government as a last resort, those who insist on it as a first resort, and many in between.

The tax reform debate involves a true challenge to the traditional definition of an economic conservative as one who eschews governmental involvement in the private economy. While I haven't endorsed the Treasury proposal, I welcome it as an important contribution to the debate over the proper role of taxes in shaping industrial and social policy.

Compassion and Government

In my view, compassion transcends definition. Feelings of concern for the poor, the disabled, and the troubled among us are shared very widely in America. Republican or Democrat, liberal or conservative, my own experience is that compassion for our neighbors is one feeling that unites us as Americans more than anything else. However, one question that sometimes divides us is the extent to which government should be used as a tool to express our compassion.

The Trustee's Fallacy

When I was a young lawyer, I learned one of the basic ethical rules applicable to attorneys and others who were selected to be trustees, guardians, or conservators of other people's money or property. It was not enough, we were taught, to invest and conserve the assets of the trust just as carefully as if it were our own money; that standard was much too loose. Instead, a higher standard was applicable when one was charged with taking care of "other people's money." Risky investments that an individual might reasonably make on his own were not acceptable for a fiduciary or trustee investing the assets of a widow or minor.

In short, the trustee was required to be more diligent in investing or spending the trust assets than he would be with his own money. To invest the trust assets as if they were the trustee's own would be to commit the Trustee's Fallacy. Even if the trustee were investing millions of his own dollars in a speculative venture, investing even a thousand dollars from the trust could be a fatal breach of his fiduciary duty.

Congress as Trustee

The problems faced by the Congress in the budget process are not that different from the problems of a trustee. In essence, we are also entrusted with spending and investing other people's money. In deciding whether to approve appropriations for a given military or domestic program, or whether to approve a tax break supposedly designed to stimulate investment, we too have to avoid the Trustee's Fallacy. By that I mean we have to remember that we are not just spending our own money but the taxpayers' money as well.

Every budgetary decision in Congress—whether it involves the MX missile, food stamps, or the investment tax credit—poses two questions: is the stated goal worthwhile, and is the method a useful and cost-effective way to accomplish that goal? Usually the second question is the tougher one. Almost all of us believe in maintaining a strong national defense, eliminating destitution, and promoting a vibrant, competitive economy. But very few of us can agree in all cases on the best way to accomplish these goals.

Every budgetary issue, then, involves not only moral issues pertaining to our national values, but difficult technical and empirical questions on which, more often than not, the evidence may be ambiguous or incomplete. This is true in military programs as well as in programs designed to eradicate poverty. But judgments and decisions have to be made even when the evidence is incomplete or inconclusive.

We are all familiar with that fact from our own lives. But in one sense, it is a mistake to apply conclusions drawn from personal experience to the political process. On a personal level, when we are motivated by compassion, we often blur the lines between the issue of what are desirable goals and the proper means to achieve those goals. Compassion can be so powerful a feeling that, faced with technical dilemmas or empirical uncertainties, we are prompted to throw up our hands and commit ourselves to do something, *anything*, to try to respond to the call of a fellow human being.

If the method chosen to feed the hungry, clothe the naked, or comfort the sick is not the most sensible or cost effective, it matters little. Indeed, it may even add to our feelings of self-worth to know not only that we gave, but that we gave without assurance that our good works would necessarily be effective. As we might say proudly to a friend, "We were aware of the existence of some doubt as to whether the money we gave would be used well, or with perfect efficiency, but we resolved the doubt against our own self-interest and gave anyway."

Without delving into the psychological morass of whether such an individual truly did resolve his doubt "against his self-interest," let me concede for the sake of argument that such an approach is praiseworthy on an individual level. The question is, what happens when such an approach is followed on the political level? The answer, I believe, is that it is a classic case of the Trustee's Fallacy.

Individual Giving and Government Largesse

It is one thing for an individual to resolve "against his self-interest" the technical and empirical questions entailed in a personal act of charity. It is quite another for a politician to resolve the same sort of issues against the "self-interest" of the American taxpayers, the people who are funding his act of selflessness.

This is not the problem of the so-called "limousine liberal" (the do-gooder who is immune, by virtue of suburban living and tax shelters, from the effects of the government policies he supports). Rather, this is the problem of sincere, compassionate public servants and political leaders who simply fail to recognize that they must meet a higher standard of care in deciding how to spend other people's money than in spending their own money, time, and resources.

In short, it is not enough to demonstrate irreproachably good intentions. The high standards required by the public trust must also be met on such mundane issues as efficacy and efficiency.

Avoidance of the Trustee's Fallacy, of course, is not a problem limited to social welfare programs. The defense budget is another area where good intentions and noble goals are sometimes expected to obviate the need for hard data and comprehensive analysis. There too, a fiscal conservative cannot forget that we have been entrusted with other people's money, and that the higher standard of a fiduciary must be met.

Restoring Trust

Whether one is dealing with the defense budget or Aid to Families With Dependent Children, avoidance of the Trustee's Fallacy is not just desirable as an ideal, it is essential if we are to preserve public trust and support. Most Americans are compassionate individuals willing to make meaningful contributions to the needs of the poor, the disabled, the sick, and the troubled. And most Americans are willing to support a strong national defense. But very few of us are so ideologically committed to the welfare state or the military-industrial complex that we are willing to endorse a blank check.

And if we Americans begin to feel we are being shortchanged by the Pentagon, the welfare departments, or the tax system, the trust on which our system depends will begin to evaporate.

That, in essence, is really what the *tax reform* debate is all about: how to maintain a tax system that is fundamentally fair and that reflects enough of a true social consensus to be a stabilizing factor in our economy and political life, rather than a source of conflict and distrust.

I believe we made good progress toward that goal in my years as Senate Finance Committee Chairman. I am sure that more work remains to be done.

Introduction: Why You Can't Afford to Ignore the Coming Tax Reforms

One of the most important federal tax bills in history is coming. And it doesn't matter whether liberals or conservatives control Congress.

In case you haven't figured it out yet, almost all the politicians we elect like to spend money. Your money, that is.

They like it so much that the federal government is spending a lot more than it raises in tax revenues. So much more that if anyone wanted to eliminate the deficit with evenly matched tax increases and spending cuts, taxes would need to be increased by about $100 billion each year for the next five years, as Exhibit 1 illustrates.

To put that incredible number into intimate terms, consider that raising $100 billion from individual and corporate income taxes would require a 25 percent increase in the average American's tax bill. For a middle-class family of four earning $30,000 and paying $3,500 in income taxes, that could mean an increase of almost $1,000!

The possibility of a major tax increase is so great that talk about "tax reform"—serious talk—is rampant. It's not hard to figure. The smart money is betting that the typical American family of four is not going to be wild about paying another $1,000 in taxes, especially when government services are being cut back.

President Reagan has announced that he's not interested in "raising" taxes. (He says he'll consider a tax increase to balance the budget only as a last resort if it's clear that no more spending cuts can be achieved.) But the President is also *very* interested in "tax reform." And for an individual taxpayer, homeowner, small businessman, or con-

Exhibit 1. Congressional estimates of tax revenues, government spending, and budget deficits (in billions).

(Fiscal Year Ending Sept 30)	1984	1985	1986	1987	1988	1989
Indiv. income tax	$302	$342	$375	$411	$454	$498
Corp. income tax	60	66	73	86	91	96
Social insurance taxes	239	268	290	311	345	372
Excise taxes:						
Windfall profit	8	7	5	5	4	4
Other	29	32	30	31	31	30
Estate & gift	6	6	5	5	5	5
Customs duties	11	13	13	14	15	15
Misc. receipts	17	18	19	19	20	21
Total	673	751	811	881	965	1042
Spending	845	929	1006	1097	1203	1305
Deficit	(172)	(178)	(195)	(216)	(238)	(263)

Source: Congressional Budget Office. *The Economic and Budget Outline; An Update.* August 1984.

sumer, some of the "tax reforms" being considered can be much more serious than a simple tax increase. In fact, "tax reform" can mean a tax increase for you, while someone else's taxes are lowered!

For almost a year, President Reagan's tax lawyers and free-market economists in the Treasury Department have worked on a plan for what they call "Fundamental Tax Reform." And they're not the only ones who have been preparing for the great tax reform debate. Democrats and Republicans in Congress have been introducing bills to "restructure" the federal income tax. And just in case that "last resort" has to be used, lobbyists for major corporations are scurrying around Washington talking about tax reform alternatives, trying to ensure that the burden of a major tax increase doesn't fall on them.

WINNERS AND LOSERS

But someone may have to pay more taxes, directly or indirectly. Explicity or implicity. Whether they realize that what they are paying is a tax, *or don't realize it!*

In case you were wondering, the corporations don't want their taxes increased by 25 percent either. And the tax-shelter salesmen could actually go out of business if too many loopholes were closed. So the Washington lobbyists will have more than enough business (thank you). If they're as good as their Gucci's, any tax increases or "reforms" that are adopted certainly won't be passed out randomly. Whatever happens, it won't be an accident. If someone else wins big, you may have to pick up more than your fair share. Unless you can afford a 25 or 30 percent tax increase, you can't afford to ignore this fight.

CAN YOU "PROFIT" FROM THE COMING TAX CHANGE?

The way our tax laws are written, the cards are clearly stacked against the average citizen. But this year could be different.

Taxpayers across the country are beginning to seriously question the taxes they pay. Of course, no one *enjoys* paying taxes. But the growing dissatisfaction with income taxes reflects much more than a simple concern with the "bottom line."

For many Americans, filing a federal income tax return has become an almost torturous experience. It's not that the tax forms are complex and difficult to understand. (They are, but that's only the first part of this economic equivalent of the Chinese water torture.) The fact is, when the IRS instructions tell you to "file Schedule A, but not Schedule C" or "skip lines 41 through 49, and go to line 50," it is almost impossible to keep from wondering about the other fellow who *does* file Schedule C, and claims a tax credit on line 41, 42, 43, 44, 45, 46, 47, or 48. What is it that those guys are getting that you're not? And do they deserve it?

The tax law is so complicated that most of us have no idea how the whole system really works and who's profiting from the hundreds of tax breaks and loopholes we skip over in filing our taxes. A few have all but given up in despair. And more than a third of us can't or won't prepare our own taxes and will pay someone else to do it instead.

People are beginning to talk about finding a better way, a simpler tax where everyone pays what he should, with no loopholes. And the politicians are listening, *very* carefully. There is a real chance now that the federal income tax could be radically altered, reformed, or even replaced with something completely different! But for every proposal that sounds "flat" or "fair" or "simple" there is more, much more, than meets the eye. That's why this tax book was written—to review where we are and how we got here, and to explain in simple terms the plans and schemes your congressperson will be talking about and actually voting on.

HOW TO USE THIS BOOK

This book is divided into three parts. Part 1 explains what "tax reform" really means, and describes some of the more prominent proposals designed to replace the income tax or to improve it.

Part 2 describes several possible strategies for surviving tax reform once you've decided where your own best interests lie.

Finally, the appendices present summary information you may want to use for quick reference.

You can, of course, start at the beginning and read straight through. But if you want to know where the "dirty parts" are . . . here's a little index of the dog-eared pages on my personal copy.

1

Why Politicians Hate to Raise Taxes but Love "Tax Reform"

Washington politicians really don't have much of an appetite for collecting or raising taxes. Unless they really and truly *have to*. And then you'd better watch out!

A politician *"forced"* to raise taxes is as dangerous as a wounded animal. Politicians don't run for office in order to vote for a tax bill. They run to get more federal aid for education, to protect us from Soviet aggression, to clean up the environment (oh yes, and to get that federal office complex built in their district). They don't bargain at all for having to raise taxes to pay for any of that stuff. And your congressman or congresswoman certainly didn't bargain to pay for an office building in someone *else's* district. That's why politicians *forced* to raise taxes are so dangerous. If there isn't enough money around to accomplish their social and political goals with a direct spending program, they will be forced to do it indirectly. They have no choice but to become "tax reformers."

The wonderful thing about being a tax reformer is that tax reform can mean almost anything you choose. In 1984, Congress decided to raise taxes—not by raising tax rates—but by a "tax reform" that consisted of closing "loopholes," including reducing the special depreciation deductions allowable for investments in apartments, offices, shopping centers, and other buildings. The new rules applied across the board, almost. An exception was granted in the Senate for investments in apartment buildings renting to low-income tenants.

Now, no direct federal expenditure was authorized or appropriated by anyone. But by simply obtaining an exemption for low-income housing, a small number of senators were able to confer a valuable benefit on the builders and developers of this one form of real estate above all others. Theoretically, the benefit was intended for the occupants of these housing units, the low-income residents themselves. The senators who voted for the exception were able to go back to their states, and to the lobbyists representing low-income housing developers, and claim credit *as if they had enacted a new federal housing program.*

In the same bill, Congress adopted a set of tough new rules preventing tax-shelter investors from claiming deductions too early, before they were properly entitled to them. A general rule was agreed to, along with a special exemption for oil-drilling tax shelters. In theory, the social policy behind this exception was to encourage exploration for oil, just as the special rule for low-income housing depreciation was intended to benefit the poor.

Depending on your own personal views, providing subsidies for oil drilling and low-income housing projects may be good or bad. The important point to remember is that these provisions were both part of the 1984 tax *reform* bill, the biggest tax reform bill in history (so far). If you are starting to think that "tax reform" can mean very different things to liberals and conservatives, to westerners and easterners, to farmers and manufacturers, you have picked up one of the most important lessons about our tax laws. There is no such thing as "good" tax policy in any absolute sense. There are only *different* tax policies.

Now don't go too far with that thought. Many things done in the name of reform can be worthwhile improvements. Just keep in mind, though, that the tax system has become much more than a way of raising revenue to pay for government programs.

THE POWER TO DESTROY . . . THE POWER TO CREATE

In 1819, in one of the earliest tax cases decided by the Supreme Court, Chief Justice John Marshall wrote that "the power to tax involves the power to destroy." Marshall was probably our greatest Supreme Court justice. Had he gone on to say that "the power to tax also involves the power to create," he would have been a true visionary.

Marshall's unforgettable phrase was *not* written about the rigors of an income-tax audit (although anyone who has been through an IRS examination feels that he or she knows instinctively what Marshall meant). The income tax as an institution in American life was a century away (although an income tax was briefly imposed during the Civil War). Marshall was writing about a tax imposed by the State of Maryland on the activities of the Bank of the United States, an arm of the federal government. If the State of Maryland could tax the federal government's activities, it could regulate them, and even impose a tax so onerous as to "destroy" or nullify the effectiveness of a federal instrumentality. (Imagine a state tax on federal inspectors enforcing civil rights laws, pollution regulations, occupational safety laws, or the 55-mile-per-hour national speed limit!) Although taxes are usually thought of as ways to raise revenues, Marshall was correct in seeing that the taxing power of the states or the federal government could be used to impose a levy so onerous as to be tantamount to a regulation forbidding, or at least severely discouraging, activities that Congress or a state legislature disapproved of.

There are a few examples of taxes used for this purpose in our current tax code. But they are unusual, and stand out by their colorful names. Consider, for example, the "Gas Guzzler Tax," imposed in 1978 on manufacturers of automobiles with low fuel-economy ratings, or the tax enacted in 1984 on "Golden Parachutes" (contracts providing generous compensation to corporate executives who "bail out" during a hostile merger or acquisition).

Despite Justice Marshall's warning—or perhaps because of it— Congress has only sparingly imposed taxes to discourage or "destroy" undesirable behavior. Instead, Congress has tended to spare the rod and spoil the child. The federal taxing power has been used not to destroy, but to create programs and implement social policies that influence the society and the economy as much, if not more, than the federal government's regulations and direct spending programs.

The Department of Housing and Urban Development's annual budget provides a case in point. In 1983 this agency, charged with executing the government's housing and urban policies, spent about $15.3 billion, a respectable sum amounting to a little less than 2 percent of the federal budget for that year. But more than twice that amount—

$40.7 billion—was "given away" by tax provisions intended to provide subsidies and incentives for homeownership. Most notable among these are the deductions for mortgage interest and property taxes on owner-occupied homes. If the special tax provisions for rental housing and rehabilitation of historic buildings are added to the pot, the contribution of the *tax* laws to federal housing and urban development policy is almost three times the total budget of the *Department* of Housing and Urban Development.

TAX GIVEAWAYS

Most of us think of tax loopholes and other special exemptions in very personal terms, primarily related to our concerns about fairness. Mainly, we think about our own tax bill (too high, not enough deductions) and someone else's tax bill, usually a corporation's (too low, too many deductions). These very legitimate personal concerns are at the heart of the growing popular interest in tax reform. But if you are concerned with fairness and want to know what you're up against, it's essential to understand the sheer magnitude of the social and economic programs that gain their financial support not from direct government spending, but from the tax code's exemptions, exceptions, and special rules.

First of all, the amount of tax money intentionally given away through the tax code has become so large that the budget experts in Congress and the Treasury Department had to invent a name for the special provisions of the income tax laws intended to create subsidies or incentives for particular industries or activities. The name sounds strange at first since it is made up of two words that most of us think of as opposites: "tax" and "expenditure." A "tax expenditure" is neither a tax nor an expenditure, exactly. The easiest way to define it might be: a special provision that "forgives" a tax liability, intentionally, as a reward for a certain kind of behavior.

Not all deductions in the tax code are tax expenditures, since we would not think of all of them as "forgiving" taxes. Many deductions are essential just to figure out the right amount of taxes due. For example, the owner of the neighborhood newsstand may sell $70,000 of newspapers this year. Since the income tax is imposed on his profits, not on his total sales, he is permitted to subtract (or deduct) the $20,000 he paid to the newspaper companies to buy the papers, and the $10,000 he paid to rent the space under his newsstand. As a result, his income is not $70,000, but $40,000, after necessary expenses have been subtracted.

If he has had a good year, with an income of $40,000, he may feel generous enough to contribute $1,000 to his favorite charity, the Home for Indigent Retired Newspaper Dealers. In figuring out his final tax liability, the newsstand owner is permitted an additional $1,000 deduction because of his gift to the home, a qualified charitable organization. That deduction has no relationship to the amount of profits or income he earned from selling newspapers. He is entitled to the deduction only because Congress decided that it was a good thing to encourage people to give to organizations like the Home for Indigent Retired Newspaper Dealers. The $20,000 of deductions for his payments to newspaper companies and the $10,000 deduction for his rent are not tax expenditures, since they are essential to computing the profits of the newsstand. The $1,000 deduction allowed for a contribution to charity is a tax expenditure, since it is a deduction designed to "forgive" part of the newsstand owner's taxes as a reward or an incentive for contributing to charity.

Because of the tax deduction for contributions to charity, the government receives less tax revenues and some charities receive more money in contributions. The effect is similar, though not identical, to what would happen if Congress had given money directly to the Home for Indigent Retired Newspaper Dealers. Although the deduction is allowed under the *tax* laws, the effect is similar to a direct federal *expenditure*. That's how the term "tax expenditure" was created.

Tax expenditures cannot only be identified, their impact on the economy—and on the federal budget—can actually be measured in dollars and cents. In fact, since 1974, the Congressional Budget Office has been required to keep an annual budget of tax expenditures. Tax expenditures have grown steadily from 1967, when they totaled less than $40 billion, to over $321 billion in 1984.

In 1982, something very dramatic occurred quietly in the tax expenditure budget.

For the first time since the records were kept, the amount of tax expenditures under the corporate income tax slightly exceeded the amount of corporate taxes actually paid. What that means is that more money was given away to American corporations in special tax breaks than the entire amount of income taxes paid by corporate America. While the corporate income tax raised $49.2 billion in 1982, a total of $55 billion was "forgiven" through tax expenditure provisions used by U.S. corporations to reduce their income tax bills. And in 1983, corporate tax expenditures outstripped corporate receipts by more than $25 billion! (For a complete list of current tax expenditures, see Appendix C.)

Restraining the use of tax expenditures in both the corporate and individual income taxes is the admitted goal of nearly all the current proposals for tax simplification and tax reform. But before you sign on the dotted line, just keep in mind that one of the biggest tax expenditures of all is the typical American homeowner's deductions for mortgage interest and property taxes!

If you are starting to wonder whether you really want "tax reform" . . . read on. It may depend on what kind of "reform" Congress and the President have in mind for you!

2

An Introduction to Flat Taxes (the One You Don't Want and the One You've Forgotten)

The most talked about idea for tax reform—and probably the least understood—has been called the "flat tax." A great deal of the confusion surrounding the flat tax is perfectly understandable, since there is really more than one flat tax plan. And several plans claim to have the virtues of being "flatter" without being "flat."

Members of Congress introducing new legislation sometimes act like overly proud new parents—the most important thing often seems to be choosing the right name for the bill. (The technical term for this is the "short title.") The would-be fathers and mothers of our future tax code have introduced the FAIR tax, the FAST tax, the SELF tax, the SIMPLIFORM, and many others. As you can see, they try to use whatever advantages in packaging they can.

It's wise to avoid the trap of judging a bill by its short title. As a starting point in understanding where we are now (and what some of the alternatives are), let's consider one "flat-tax" you almost certainly don't want, another you've forgotten about, and a third that you may want, depending on how much tax you're currently paying.

THE "I DIDN'T MEAN *THAT* FLAT" TAX

How flat a tax do you want? If fairness and flatness are not the same, how "steep" should a fair tax be? These are some of the questions politicians and scholars are asking about the tax system.

One way to start answering for yourself is to consider the flattest tax of all. It's called here the "I Didn't Mean *That* Flat" Tax, since that's how many people react when they hear of it. But this sort of tax, a per-capita tax (also called a head tax, poll tax, and capitation), was one of the forms of federal taxation contemplated by the U.S. Constitution back in 1789.

In 1983, the cost of running the federal government amounted to $808 billion (about 25 percent of the Gross National Product). With 234 million people living in the United States, a *per-capita* tax of $3,450 for every man, woman, and child could pay for the entire federal government with no income taxes, social security taxes, estate taxes, or customs duties.

The tax system would be very simple. The tax form would have only one line, and everyone would know exactly what everyone else was paying: $3,450.

The tax system would not discourage (or encourage) savings, investment, or work, since nothing anyone could do would raise or lower their tax bill. Of course, between 20 and 30 million families would be completely unable to pay their taxes, and millions more would have only meager amounts of after-tax income.

No one is seriously suggesting the adoption of a per-capita tax. But thinking about it for a moment may put some focus on the issues involved in the tax debate.

Obviously, no one expects poor people to pay the government $3,450 each year, before spending money on food, clothing, and shelter. And almost no one would approve of a tax system that asked the typical family of four earning $26,000 to pay $13,800 in "head taxes" ($3,450 per family member) while the very unusual family of four earning $200,000 paid the same $13,800. Even though everyone would be treated the same (one definition of fairness), most Americans wouldn't think of that as a fair tax system.

Under today's tax laws, the typical family of four earning $26,000 pays about $4,500 in income and social security taxes (less than half of their per-capita share), and anyone with no income pays nothing. But the cost of running the federal government ($3,450 per person) still has to be paid. So—somebody else has to pay more than $3,450 per person. It's the job of the tax law to figure out who pays, and how much.

In contrast to the perfectly flat, perfectly impossible per-capita tax, the income tax is supposed to be a method of sharing the cost of government in accordance with each individual's ability to pay. But figuring out "ability to pay" is not as simple as it may sound.

The cost of government could be paid for by taxing only individuals actually earning an income. And it could be shared by requiring everyone to pay a fixed percentage of their income. This "flat rate" tax on income is one of the flat tax proposals being discussed. Although it may sound like a revolutionary proposal, we have been living with a flat tax very much like that for more than 40 years.

THE "FORGOTTEN" FLAT TAX

The per-capita tax is perfectly flat and perfectly impossible to implement. But since 1937, the Social Security System has been paid for by a flat tax imposed on employers and employees.

It's called here the "Forgotten" Flat Tax since many people who think about proposals for a flat-rate income tax forget about this flat-rate tax on wages. Today, the social security tax is a flat tax on wages and salaries, with about 7 percent paid by the employer and about 7 percent paid by the employee. (Self-employed individuals like doctors and lawyers pay the entire tax themselves, but pay at a flat rate slightly less than 12 percent.)

This flat-rate tax on wages is also very simple to understand and administer. Workers have virtually no paperwork or forms since the tax is easy to figure and is withheld from wages. There are no deductions or tax shelters, and everyone has a pretty good idea what everyone else is paying. (A few loopholes may appear from time to time. But they are usually easy to close because they were not put in the system intentionally, as a way of providing a hidden federal subsidy.) The problems of the per-capita tax don't exist: children and retired people without wage incomes pay no social security tax. Nor do the unemployed, the disabled, and husbands or wives who choose not to work outside the home.

Almost everyone would agree that the tax burden is shared more fairly under the flat-rate social security tax than under the "I Didn't Mean *That* Flat" Tax. For example, a teacher earning a salary of

$15,000 pays around $1,050 (with a matching contribution from the school district), whereas an engineer earning twice as much ($30,000) pays twice as much in taxes ($2,100) with another matching contribution from the employer. And a married couple, where the husband and wife both earn $30,000, each pay about $2,100 for a grand total of $4,200 on a total income of $60,000, again with a matching contribution by each employer.

Speaking of marriage, this tax has no marriage penalty or bonus and no discrimination against unmarried people. And it doesn't discourage a husband or wife from going to work because the other spouse is in a high-income tax bracket. Everyone is in the same tax bracket under the social security tax.

The social security tax is not a true flat-rate income tax for several reasons. First and foremost, the amount of wages subject to the flat 14 percent is capped at around $40,000—a limit that "flattens" the tax and brings it closer to a per-capita tax. The cap means that the maximum tax for any wage earner is no higher than about $2,800 paid by the employee and another $2,800 paid by the employer. The main reason for these limits is the fact that social security tax is devoted to the social security retirement, health insurance, and disability system, which has limits on the amount of retirement and disability benefits that can be paid out. But the cap could, conceivably, be removed on the tax side only, as a way of raising additional revenue—in which case a corporate executive earning $200,000 would pay $14,000 with a matching $14,000 contribution from the employer.

To raise the $808 billion used to run the government in 1983, a flat tax on wages alone would have to be set at almost 50 percent—25 percent paid by the employer and 25 percent paid by the employee. This very high tax rate illustrates why the "Forgotten" Flat Tax of the social security system would not be a true flat-rate income tax even if the $40,000 cap on taxable wages were removed. The "Forgotten" Flat Tax also "forgets" to tax an important source of income: earnings from individual savings and investment.

THE "REALLY FLAT, TRUE INCOME TAX"

Unlike the flat social security tax on wages and salaries, the "Really Flat, True Income Tax" would also levy an annual tax on the income earned on stocks and bonds and other investments. Taxing the earnings from an individual's savings and investment—along with any wage and salary income—seems at first to be a straightforward, uncomplicated idea. But when you bring it down to real cases, Americans sometimes have confusing thoughts and conflicting feelings. The "Really Flat, True Income Tax" would tax not only wages and salaries, but all interest income from money market funds and corporate bonds, dividends and capital gains from stocks, and gains from passive investments in oil wells, apartment buildings, and cattle herds (to name a few of the more popular "tax-sheltered" investments). A true income tax at a 14 percent flat rate would raise about as much as our current income tax, and a 20 percent flat rate would be more than enough to balance the budget (as long as the "forgotten" social security tax on wages is retained).

Imagining a flat-rate, 20 percent tax on "true income" is a good way to face up to the almost schizophrenic feelings Americans often have about taxing the income from savings and investment. Imagine Jim Johnson, a newly hired construction worker, married with one child, who earns $30,000. His wife takes care of the child at home and keeps expenses down, so the family is able to put away some money for the proverbial rainy day, or perhaps for the child's college education. In his first year on the job, after paying a 20 percent flat-rate income tax of $6,000, he has $24,000 and spends only $22,000, putting $2,000 into a short-term money market fund that pays 10 percent interest.

The next year Jim earns $30,000 again, and the $2,000 he saved has grown to $2,200. His new tax bill is not $6,000 but $6,040, because the 20 percent flat rate-income tax is imposed on his interest income of $200. (This, of course, is exactly how our current tax system works except for the fact that the tax rates get higher and higher as annual income goes up.)

When Jim fills out his tax return, he'll probably grumble about paying the extra $40. It wasn't easy to save $2,000 on his income, and the politicians in Washington keep talking about how we should be saving more as a nation and consuming less. The extra $40 isn't really that much money, but the galling thing is that it feels like *double* taxation. He already paid a 20 percent tax when he earned $30,000 last year, and now he has to pay taxes again on the money he earned from saving part of his salary. Jim grumbles every year, and he pays the tax. But he wonders whether the money he earns from savings shouldn't be free from this "double tax."

Now imagine Jim's employer, the Phillips Construction Company. The firm is run by the general manager, Frank Ferello, who is an employee like Jim, except that Frank earns $100,000.

Frank has been in the business for 20 years, since old Mr. Phillips started the company. After Mr. Phillips died, his two sons, Biff and Tad Phillips, inherited the company. Biff and Tad pretty much let Frank Ferello make the day-to-day decisions, since they are not really interested in the company—except for the $400,000 profits the firm makes each year. They each report $200,000 in income from the Phillips Construction Company, and (under our hypothetical flat-rate income tax) pay a 20 percent tax of $40,000 on the income from their investment in the company, leaving them with $160,000 each to spend or invest. Frank Ferello also pays 20 percent on his salary of $100,000. Here's what their tax bills would look like:

Taxpayer	Income	Tax	Percentage of Income Paid in Tax
Jim Johnson	$ 30,200	$ 6,040	20
Frank Ferello	$100,000	$20,000	20
Biff Phillips	$200,000	$40,000	20
Tad Phillips	$200,000	$40,000	20

There would be no deductions for home mortgage interest, charitable contributions, or medical expenses. And no tax shelters for Jim (like an Individual Retirement Account) or Frank, Biff, and Tad (like an oil-drilling tax shelter).

Biff and Tad don't like paying taxes any more than the rest of us, but their eyes really light up when they hear some economists and politicians agreeing with Jim that the tax on savings and investment income is a "double tax" that should be reduced or eliminated. Without a tax on savings and investment income, they would earn $200,000 each year, and pay nothing in federal income taxes!

Although many of us sympathize with Jim's frustration at paying an additional $40 in taxes on his hard-earned savings, we may not feel that Biff and Tad should avoid paying $40,000 in taxes on their investment income from the Phillips Construction Company. In fact, some of us feel that the "idle rich" should pay higher taxes on their investment income than Jim Johnson pays on his savings.

How Should Savings and Investment Be Taxed?

The ambivalent feelings many of us have about taxing the income from savings and investment are not hard to reconcile when we think only about exaggerated stereotypes like hard-working Jim Johnson and the good-for-nothing Phillips boys. Thinking only about these comic strip examples, we can see why Congress made a distinction (from 1970 until 1981) between investment income and salaries.

Between 1970 and 1981, investment income was taxable at rates as high as 70 percent, while wages and salaries could not be taxed any more heavily than 50 percent. That distinction may be momentarily satisfying until one remembers Frank Ferello, the General Manager of Phillips Construction, who may be saving money from his $100,000 salary to invest in his own company or to buy out the Phillips brothers' shares. Frank might actually run a more efficient operation if he had a stake in the company. And the idea of a hard-working employee saving to build or buy his own business is a big part of the American dream. The response of Congress to the situation of the Frank Ferello's of the country included several of the special tax deductions and exclusions that have made our tax code as complex as it is, including favorable rules for employee stock options and for stock purchase plans (rules that were substantially amended in 1964, 1969, 1976, 1981, 1982, and 1984).

While Congress was tinkering with the tax rate on investment income in a few sympathetic cases like employee stock options, it was hard put to resist providing just a few more breaks for activities that were having a little trouble attracting investment capital, like rehabilitation of low-income housing (1969), export sales (1971), loans to college students (1976), preservation of historic structures (1976), hiring the disadvantaged (1977), energy conservation (1978), alternative fuels (1980), intercity bus transportation (1980), reforestation (1980), research and development (1981), and public utilities (1981)—to name just a few.

The "Really Flat, True Income Tax" would tax all earnings from savings and investment and not distinguish between Jim Johnson, Frank Ferello, and Biff and Tad Phillips. It also wouldn't create tax shelters (or incentives) for investors in low-income housing, or oil drilling, or the production of alternative fuels.

PUTTING IT IN PERSPECTIVE

So far, this chapter has thrown around a lot of ideas. Some of them may be a little new, and a few may be more than a little perplexing. Let's try to focus the discussion a bit. First of all, nobody wants (or could live with) a perfectly flat tax that treats everyone identically. But a flat tax that requires everyone to pay the same flat percentage of their income is very realistic, since we've been living with a flat tax on wages for more than 40 years.

The social security tax on wages is simple, and for many people relatively painless, since it is taken out of our weekly paychecks. There are no widespread stories of "loopholes" or rich people avoiding the tax, mainly because it is not filled with exemptions and special deductions to encourage different kinds of behavior. One of the reasons the social security tax is so simple is that it completely ignores income from savings and investment, and only taxes wages paid to employees and the incomes of self-employed individuals like physicians, accountants, and attorneys. But a flat tax on wages alone might not be fair and would have to be set at a very high 50 percent rate to pay for the cost of government. So that isn't a very likely scenario. In contrast, a flat tax on *all* sources of income could easily be set at a 20 percent rate or even lower. But that would raise a lot of questions about how investment income should be taxed.

Most of the complexity of the tax laws springs from special rules about the taxation of savings and investment income. This complexity results in part from the very mixed feelings many of us have about savings (good) and investment (very good) and what results when some people save a lot and make smart investments (wealth).

FAIRNESS VERSUS FLATNESS

The social security tax is "flat" and the income tax is not. Which type of tax is a fairer tax, and which should be the model for the ideal tax? Let's look at the simple case of three individual wage earners. One earns $20,000, the second earns $75,000, and the third earns $200,000.

A flat-rate tax would produce the following tax burdens:

Income	Tax	Percent of Income Paid in Tax
$ 20,000	$ 4,000	20
$ 75,000	$15,000	20
$200,000	$40,000	20

The more the individual earns, the more he or she pays. And the tax burden is a flat percentage of income. In comparison, the current federal income tax (assuming that our hypothetical friends are married with only one spouse earning an income, have no children, foolishly live in rented apartments, claim the standard deduction, and don't invest in tax shelters) would produce the following results:

Income	Tax	Percent of Income Paid in Tax
$ 20,000	$ 2,106	11
$ 75,000	$20,628	28
$200,000	$80,400	40

Is it "fair" to ask the person earning $200,000 to pay 40 percent of his or her income in taxes, while the person earning $75,000 pays only 28 percent, and the person earning $20,000 pays only 11 percent?

Our current income tax laws seem to say, "Yes, it is fair." Essentially, the theory of a "progressive" or "graduated" income tax is that wealthier people should not only pay more but that they should pay much more (that is, a higher percentage of income than lower income individuals). But many of the current tax reform proposals say "No."

Of course, almost no one will come out and say that wealthier people should pay less taxes and lower income people should pay more taxes. Generally, flat taxes (or the tax plans that are "flatter" without being truly "flat") are advocated as being simpler and fairer, because their simplicity allows us to be sure that everyone is at least paying the same, flat percentage of income with no loopholes. Some public opinion polls indicate that many Americans do favor "graduated" or "unflat" income taxes. The curious thing is that there is almost no audible criticism of the "flat" social security tax as being "unfair."

The reason for this may be related to the purpose of the tax. The social security tax is used to pay for social security benefits, which, like the tax itself, are closely related to the amount of an individual's wages. There is a close tie in people's minds between the tax burden and the benefits of the social security system. The income tax, however, supports the entire range of government services other than social security and Medicare, which are separately funded by the social security tax. And almost 40 percent of this $626 billion package of government service goes to pay for national defense.

When we think of having to pay the very large amounts needed to support an army, a navy, and an airforce to defend the entire nation, the notion that wealthier individuals should pay "much more" seems to win out. Indeed the most significant increases in the federal income tax accompanied the two world wars. Even so, it can be argued that the very wealthy gain as much from the domestic tranquility provided by the social security system as they do from the military. And the average American, who will have to fight in a war that might break out, may gain much more from having a well-equipped military than the majority of wealthy individuals who may be well beyond draft age.

In short, the issue of fairness versus flatness is not cut and dried. More important, the answers given by our current system are not engraved in stone. The federal income tax has not been around continuously as long as the airplane. And, like developments in aviation since the Wright Brothers took off at Kitty Hawk, the current system bears little resemblance to the original provisions of the Revenue Act of 1913. That tax had rates that ranged from one percent on incomes in excess of $3,000, to a maximum rate of 7 percent, which was applicable only to incomes in excess of $500,000! Today the rates start at 11 percent for incomes over $2,300 and rise to 50 percent for individuals earning more than $81,800 and couples earning more than $162,400.

But much more revealing than these numbers are the figures on how many more people have to file an annual tax return. Out of 97 million people living in the United States in 1913 the number of individual income tax returns filed totaled less than half a million. That was less than one-half of one percent of the population. By 1968, the population had just about doubled to 200 million. But the number of individual tax returns filed had increased more than 200 times to 73 million. This year, more than 95 million Americans will file individual tax returns, and soon the number will reach 100 million. (The IRS has not announced whether they will be giving a prize to the lucky man or woman who, one of these years, files the hundred-millionth tax return.) The income tax is dramatically more pervasive and intrusive than its original proponents ever imagined. As the next chapter reveals, some people think it's time to go back to the drawing board.

3

A Tax on Spending?

In one of Woody Allen's films, the character played by Woody Allen is cryogenically frozen, after complications arise in a routine gallbladder operation in the late 1970s. He is awakened by a group of physicians 200 years later in a high-tech, futuristic society. When offered food, he asks for wheat germ, tiger's milk, and other 20th-century "health foods," only to be informed by the doctors that modern experts now know that eating chocolate layer cake and sirloin steak and smoking cigarettes is the way to keep calories off, lungs clear, and cholesterol low.

The "progressive" supporters of the 1913 income tax might experience a similar jolt of "future shock" listening to the current tax reform debate. Popular dissatisfaction with the income tax, as well as the cogent arguments of some economists, are reviving interest in the very sort of tax the reforms of 1913 were intended to replace: a tax on consumer spending or "consumption." If one of these early tax reformers had fallen asleep in 1913 and awakened in 1985 to a discussion of "consumption taxes," he might need to be reassured that no one was seriously suggesting that tuberculosis victims be taxed! Could he be convinced that a national tax on the goods and services *consumed* by individuals was any less horrible than a tax on chronic diseases?

HOW WE INHERITED THE "PROGRESSIVE" INCOME TAX

The federal income tax on individuals enacted in 1913, together with the corporate tax adopted in 1909, were part of a "tax reform" movement that struggled for more than 20 years to overcome political and constitutional objections to an annual tax on individual incomes. At the turn of the century, the federal government collected revenue almost entirely from tariffs (customs duties on imported goods) and "sin" taxes on tobacco and alcoholic beverages. The movement to replace these tariffs and excise taxes with a tax on income was prompted by a growing concern with the concentration of money and power among the wealthy.

Import tariffs, which not only raised revenue but also protected American manufacturers from foreign competition, were thought to be responsible for encouraging the growth of mammoth corporate empires. The concentration of wealth and power among large corporations and wealthy individuals was viewed by many as a threat to the middle classes, and to democratic government. The "progressive" income tax was one of many reforms of the "progressive" movement that included laws against business monopolies, labor laws, railroad regulations, and measures to protect the poor and underprivileged.

REFORM REARS ITS HEAD AGAIN

Many of the fundamental tax reform proposals being talked about today reflect an almost complete turnabout in attitudes concerning the income tax.

It is not hard to see why middle-class sentiment has changed over the last 70 years. Turn-of-the-century supporters of the income tax may have been concerned about the high concentration of the nation's income among the very wealthiest of American families. In 1896, more than 10 percent of the nation's income was earned by the wealthiest 2 percent of American families. Fair enough. The 1913 tax law required only the wealthy—less than one percent of the population—to file a tax return.

Seventy years later, the 83 million households in America filed more than 95 million individual income tax returns, and more than half of the income taxes collected were paid by taxpayers with incomes less than $40,000. Only 10 percent of the individual income taxes collected in 1981 were paid by taxpayers with incomes greater than $200,000.

Before you jump to conclusions and skip to the chapter entitled "Soaking The Rich," keep in mind that the 175,000 wealthiest taxpayers in America paid an average income tax bill of $135,000 that year. That's a far cry from the $3,450 per-capita cost of running the government, no matter how you look at it. These individuals, earning an average income of $450,000, represented less than one-tenth of one percent of the population and paid about 8 percent of the nation's individual income tax bill. In short, while the rich are paying a significant amount in taxes, the income tax has become predominantly a *middle-class* tax.

On the corporate side, the tax bite in 1909 was only one percent of corporate profits with an exemption of $5,000 for each company. That was like having the government be a one percent partner in each and every American corporation. Today, the tax rate is up to 46 percent. (No exemptions are allowed, but there is a small business provision giving lower rates for the first $100,000 of corporate profits.) The government is no longer a one percent partner but a 46 percent partner with corporate America. Although almost 3 million corporate returns are filed each year, more than half of the corporate taxes are paid by 3,000 of the largest companies, whose assets exceeded $250 million a piece. Today's corporate income tax, paid largely by mammoth corporations, may seem perfectly in tune with the "progressive" sentiments of 1913. But there are critics who blame this tax on business profits for the present decline in the productivity and growth of American companies, as well as the diminished competitiveness of the United States in international trade. Let's see what the younger generation of tax reformers have in mind!

THE PEOPLE VS. THE EXPERTS

The real impetus for serious consideration of a national tax based on what people spend, rather than on what they earn, is not coming from the tax "experts." There are some economists and scholars who believe that the income tax should be replaced with a tax based on what people spend. But the idea is getting political attention only because of the increasing evidence that the tax reform "experts" are out of touch with the views of the American people.

Most tax reform "experts" say that the progressive income tax is "fair" because it is based on each individual's ability to pay taxes. Higher income means a greater ability to pay, which should be reflected (they say) in a higher tax bill. Taxes on consumer spending, like the retail sales taxes levied by most of the 50 states, are considered by the experts to be "unfair," compared to the progressive income tax.

But the experts haven't been doing a very good job at reminding the American people what they are supposed to think about the taxes they pay. According to a *New York Times*/CBS News Poll conducted in 1983, only 41 percent of the public feels that the federal income tax is "fair." More significant are reports of polls conducted by the Advisory Commission on Intergovernmental Relations since 1972, asking the public to identify the "least fair" tax. Asked in 1984 to select among the federal income tax, state income taxes, state sales taxes, and local property taxes, those polled gave the booby prize to the federal income tax. Thirty-six percent said the federal income tax was "the worst tax" while only 15 percent said the state sales tax was "the worst tax—that is, the least fair."

In 1980, a Gallup Poll conducted for the U.S. Chamber of Commerce asked if people would prefer an income tax reduction, a sales tax reduction, or a tax cut evenly divided between the two. Forty-two percent said they would choose the income tax reduction. Thirty-six percent wanted an evenly divided tax cut, and only 14 percent opted for the sales tax reduction.

THE "ONE DAY AT A TIME" FLAT TAX

These survey results are a large part of the reason serious consideration is being given to the "One Day at a Time" Flat Tax. That's the name given here to proposals for a national sales tax. The name is descriptive of how it would work. Every consumer purchase would be subject to a national tax equal to a flat percentage of the sales price. If the tax rate were 10 percent, the purchase of a Mercedes sports coupe costing $45,000 would generate a tax of $4,500. The purchase of a small, stripped down, fuel-efficient Ford Escort costing $6,000 would produce a tax of $600. And for every gallon of gasoline saved by driving the Ford Escort, the driver would not only save $1.20 at the pump, but he or she would also save 12 cents in federal taxes.

Each individual's tax burden would be a flat percentage of the amount of money spent on consumer goods and services. Instead of filing a complicated tax return on April 15, the individual would pay "one day at a time," with no paperwork or record-keeping required. For the average taxpayer, the "One Day at a Time" Flat Tax represents a quantum leap toward simplification. Other advantages (and disadvantages) depend on how high the flat tax rate is set and what other taxes can be either eliminated or reduced sharply.

Predictions of the amount of money to be collected from a national sales tax vary, since almost everyone assumes that many items would either be exempted or taxed at a lower rate. Most state sales taxes exempt housing, domestic services, food furnished to employees, medical supplies, foreign travel, insurance premiums, and financial services. Many states also exclude food consumed in the home, medical expenses, household utilities, tobacco, gasoline, and private-school tuition. The most comprehensive sales tax possible would apply across the board to almost $2.3 trillion of consumer spending. A national sales tax containing the same exemptions generally found in most states would apply to almost $1.8 trillion in consumer spending.

That means that a 10 percent sales tax could have raised between $180 billion and $230 billion in 1984, and a 20 percent sales tax could have raised between $360 billion and $460 billion. What these numbers are really saying is that a 20 percent national sales tax could completely replace the entire individual and corporate income tax. If less radical surgery were desired, a 10 percent sales tax with modest exemptions could completely eliminate income taxation for all taxpayers with annual incomes under $50,000. That would relieve about 90 million people from the rigors of April 15, and require income taxes to be paid only by the 5 million wealthiest taxpayers in the country.

As you can see, the "One Day at a Time" Flat Tax is a proven, simple, and extremely powerful fiscal tool. It's not surprising that it has engendered skepticism from conservatives who believe the tax would be used to increase wasteful government spending—as well as from liberals who believe the tax is "unfair" to lower income taxpayers.

Fairness: One Day at a Time?

Let's look at the "fairness" issue. At a minimum, fairness seems to require that people with absolutely no ability to pay taxes should not have to pay taxes. That's why, regardless of its simplicity, we all reject the "I Didn't Mean *That* Flat" Tax which would demand a flat $3,450 from every man, woman, and child in the nation.

Poor people would not be exempt from a national sales tax, although certain basic goods and services like food and medical care could be excluded across the board. But even today, without a national sales tax, the government already has in place programs like food stamps and Medicaid to provide bare necessities to the very poor. It would be simple enough to increase these outlays by 10 percent to compensate for a 10 percent sales tax. For very low-income wage earners, part of their social security taxes could be refunded. This, too, is already being done, in effect, through a special income tax credit called the "earned income tax credit." Low-income elderly and disabled individuals living on fixed incomes could also be given benefits similar to food stamps or the "earned income tax credit" by a cash grant.

This may sound like an apologetic admission that a national sales tax would be intolerable to the poor unless a massive federal welfare bureaucracy were maintained and possibly expanded. But *think again*. Today, families at the official poverty level already pay between 6 and 12 percent of their incomes to the federal government in taxes! In 1984, the poverty level for a family of four was $10,613. That's the income that might be earned by a couple with two children where one spouse works full time at the federal minimum wage of $3.35 per hour and the other spouse works a little over half time. In 1984, that family was required to pay $711 in social security payroll taxes and $365 in income taxes, taking into account the special earned income tax credit. The grand total was $1,076, or slightly over 10 percent of the family's income. In short, if a national sales tax were to replace part of the income or social security taxes, it is possible that only relatively modest adjustments would be required to keep the tax burden on lower income families at a tolerable level.

What about middle- and upper-income families? Let's assume that Congress replaced the existing federal income taxes on individuals and corporations with a broad-based, 20 percent sales tax. Middle- and upper-income families would be taxed at a flat percentage rate, but only on what they spent, not on what they earned. In other words, savings and investment would be exempt from taxes until the money was used to buy something.

We know why the tax experts say this would be an unfair tax. Generally speaking, wealthier families do spend considerably more than lower and middle-income families, and they would pay more taxes under a national sales tax. But the wealthy also tend to save a larger part of their income as an investment for the future. For example, a family of four earning $20,000 might spend all but $2,000 and pay a 20 percent tax on $18,000 of consumer purchases. That would amount to $3,600. The higher income family earning $50,000 might be able to save a little bit more, spend only $42,000, and pay a sales tax of $8,400. But the very wealthy family earning $200,000 might live quite well on $150,000 and save $50,000. Their sales tax burden would be $30,000.

Although the tax burden is clearly increasing with increasing income, the highest income family is paying only 15 percent of their income in taxes, while the lower income family is paying 18 percent. Opponents of this tax say it is even less fair than a flat tax on income would be, since the higher income family is paying a lower percentage in taxes than the lower income family. Of course, the higher income family is probably saving in order to spend the money on something, so a sales tax will eventually be paid when the money is spent. Even if the money is given away to children or passed on at death, it will be taxed as soon as it is spent. In the long run, the income will be spent and taxed. So what's the problem?

Earn Now, Pay Later?

"In the long run," a famous economist once said, "We are all dead." Despite all the rhetoric about the value of savings and investment and the talk about encouraging savings with special tax provisions, some people are suspicious about wealthy people accumulating large fortunes over long periods of time. This suspicion is part of the reason we have a tax on income, rather than on spending. Part of the suspicion is that wealthy people will accumulate large fortunes and come to control massive economic empires. Part of it is simply fear of the unknown— suspicion that a tax only levied some time in the future could be avoided, while a tax on income will be paid today with certainty. (There are also some people who believe that merely earning money, without spending it, provides a measure of happiness and security, which is something that ought to be taxed on an annual basis.)

But why then do public opinion polls reveal that more people believe the income tax is "the worst tax, the least fair?" Federal income taxes are higher than most sales taxes, and a 20 percent sales tax might quickly be elevated to the exalted position of "the worst tax." Another reason may be a contradiction inherent in the income tax: most people seem to approve of the deductions and exclusions contained in the income tax—like the mortgage interest deduction, charitable contribution deduction, and exclusion of interest on municipal bonds. But when they find out that a wealthy person is using the tax code to reduce his or her income taxes, they feel a little less certain that the tax is fair. That may be because tax returns are kept confidential, and no one knows for sure what the other fellow is paying. With a sales tax, more people believe that everyone is paying a reasonable amount, because they can see it with their own eyes. That raises a very provocative question: Is it better to have a tax system that *seems* fair to a majority of Americans, or a tax that the economists and political scientists tell us is fair?

A TAX ON DRUG DEALERS?

The strongest argument for moving to a tax system that relies less on income taxes and more on sales taxes may be the so-called underground economy. The IRS thinks that about $100 billion a year in income taxes are not paid because of under-reported income or overstated deductions. That figure includes only a small amount, less than $10 billion, attributed to illegal activities like drug trafficking and prostitution. The real amount may be dozens of times greater, since the IRS has no real way of judging the size of the illegal sector. To understand the helplessness of the income tax in the illegal economy, you may want to take a little quiz on your knowledge of the tax code.

> A drug dealer buys $10,000 worth of cocaine, packages the drugs in plastic bags costing $5, incurs telephone expenses of $25, and retails the drugs for $50,000. His taxable income is:
>
> A. $50,000 (the amount he received for the drugs)
>
> B. $40,000 (the amount he received for the drugs, minus what he paid for the drugs)
>
> C. $39,970 (the amount he received for the drugs, minus what he paid for the drugs and his business expenses)
>
> D. Nothing

If you chose "A" you fail the quiz. Imposing a tax on $50,000 would be a tax on sales or gross receipts, not income. The right answer is "B," but you get half credit if you chose "C" or "D."

Traditional income tax principles tell us that the tax is imposed only on profits, which is why anyone answering "C" gets half credit. But when the United States Tax Court reached that decision in 1981, Congress was outraged by the appearance of allowing a tax deduction for drug dealers. That's why Congress passed a law preventing drug dealers from deducting even ordinary business expenses like the cost of telephone bills and plastic bags. That's why the correct answer is "B."

Believe it or not, the Congress *didn't* disallow the deductions for the cost of the drugs. The fear was that taxing the gross receipts of a business without allowing an offset for the cost of inventory would not be a tax on "income" and would be unconstitutional. That's why "A" is the wrong answer. (It also begins to explain why the income tax is so complex!)

There's no *legal* basis whatsoever for "D." But if you chose that, you get half credit for "street smarts!" Everyone knows that illegal drug dealers don't file tax returns voluntarily disclosing how much they paid for telephone bills, plastic bags, and inventory. From the pragmatic perspective, "D" is the only right answer.

Of course, drug dealers also wouldn't charge any sales taxes for cocaine, barbiturates, or marijuana. But when a drug dealer purchased a red Mercedes sports coupe for $45,000, when a pimp purchased a white Cadillac for $20,000, and when a loan shark purchased some brass knuckles for $5.95, a 10 percent sales tax would collect $4,500, $2,000, and 59 cents. That may be more than these unsavory characters are contributing today.

THE "INVISIBLE" FLAT TAX

Another reason why taxes on consumer spending are getting attention in Washington is the concern voiced by many economists, businessmen, and politicians that the income tax system discourages savings and investment. When they really want to impress you with the point, they talk about "capital formation." It's pretty much the same thing. But when you hear anyone talk about "capital formation," be sure to take a close look at how much they want to reduce taxes on business!

The smart money isn't betting on the adoption of a national retail sales tax anytime soon. But that's really more a matter of "packaging" than substance. A national sales tax is simple and straightforward and has many advantages over existing income taxes. But it is so straightforward that it would probably upset too many people—ranging from state governors (who like sales taxes so much they want them reserved for the states) to liberals who believe that preserving the income tax is the only feasible way to redistribute wealth from the very rich to the middle class and the poor.

In the meantime, the income tax remains complex, seemingly unfair, and arguably a drag on "capital formation." Many of the people who would really like to see a national sales tax have shifted their sights to what may be a more politically realistic target: the "Invisible" Flat Tax, and its cousin, the "Disguised Invisible" Flat Tax.

The Invisible Flat Tax is the name given here to a tax that is used throughout the European Common Market. Its proper name is the "value-added tax," or VAT, for short. In its most common form, the VAT is very similar to a national sales tax with two major exceptions. First, unlike a sales tax which is collected in one lump sum when a gourmet meal is served at a fancy French restaurant, the VAT is collected in pieces: one piece when the green beans are sold by the farmer to the grocer, another piece when they are sold to the restaurant owner, the final piece when the check is presented by the waiter to a hopefully satisfied patron.

The taxes paid by the farmer are passed on in the price paid by the grocer, and the grocer's tax is added to the price paid by the restaurant owner and charged to the patron. But each taxpayer also gets a rebate for the taxes paid earlier in the chain. The net effect of a 10 percent VAT is no different than a 10 percent retail sales tax.

The purpose of this elaborate approach is primarily to keep tax cheating to a minimum. If the grocer or farmer fails to pay his taxes, the full VAT will still be imposed on the customer's bill. No rebate will be available for the restaurant owner since taxes weren't properly paid further up the chain. The second reason for the elaborate chain of taxes and rebates is to facilitate exemptions for goods that are not sold at retail (like the restaurant's table setting), but are used to manufacture or market goods or services sold at retail. Under a retail sales tax the same goal is accomplished by the restaurant owner claiming an exemption for purchases of silverware, napkins, chairs, and tables.

The second major difference between a sales tax and a value-added tax can be illustrated by a comedy sketch performed on American television by British comedian Benny Hill. Portraying an obnoxious French waiter, the British comic presents an extravagant bill to an annoyed customer. The customer asks, "Does this include the V-A-T?"

The answer, "Yes, but not the T-I-P."

A VAT, of course, is not voluntary like a waiter's tip. But unlike a 15 percent tip or service charge, the VAT is generally not even disclosed on the customer's bill. Instead it is built into the purchase price. Calling this a "hidden" tax seems to imply a moral judgment about the lawmakers who designed the tax. But it is certainly fair to call it an "invisible" flat tax. Unlike the "One Day at a Time" national sales tax, the Invisible Flat Tax is a sales tax that consumers may not even realize they are paying.

A national sales tax is not voluntary (like a waiter's tip), but the customer is aware he is paying a tax, which may have political consequences that bear some resemblance to a customer's tipping habits. If "customers" are unhappy with what the government is doing with their money, they may vote to reduce the size of the "tip" they pay the government (or to replace the "waiter").

One of the arguments in favor of both the national sales tax and the VAT is that they can be used to stimulate exports and discourage imports without violating existing international trade agreements. Both of these taxes can be imposed when an American buys an imported Toyota Corolla and forgiven when a Ford Escort is sold abroad. But this benefit arises only if the VAT, or national sales tax, is adopted as a replacement for the income tax on corporations, or other taxes that are reflected in the price of goods sold. (And even then, the impact of a VAT is disputed.) Our international trade agreements do not permit us to forgive corporate income taxes on goods sold abroad, but they do allow forgiveness of sales taxes and VAT taxes.

THE "DISGUISED INVISIBLE" FLAT TAX

In most European countries, the Invisible Flat Tax has not replaced the income tax. But one of the most prominent tax reform proposals before Congress is a bill that would do just that. Legislation introduced in the 97th and 98th Congress by Democratic Senator Dennis De Concini of Arizona would repeal Section 1 through Section 1564 of the Internal Revenue Code and replace those 844 pages with an 8-page document consisting of only 10 separate provisions. According to its authors, Dr. Alvin Rabushka and Dr. Robert Hall of Stanford University, the complete individual and business tax forms could each fit on a postcard.

This flat 19 percent tax on businesses and individuals is called here the "Disguised Invisible" Flat Tax. The name suggests that with the Hall-Rabushka flat tax there is both more, and less, than meets the eye. The Disguised Invisible Flat Tax is just what its name suggests. It is an "invisible" flat tax (that is, a value-added tax on consumed goods and services) that has been disguised to look like something else. The disguise is quite intriguing. But just remember that this tax is almost the equivalent of a flat 19 percent sales tax. Let's take a close look at the disguise.

The Business Tax

The first half of the Disguised Invisible Income Tax is a flat, 19 percent tax imposed on every business in the country, whether operated as a corporation, a partnership, or a sole proprietorship. This is really not a corporate income tax, but a sort of value-added tax.

The business tax is imposed on the "profits" of the company, figured in a simple, but unusual way. The business simply adds up all of the cash it has received in sales and subtracts all of the cash it spent on the business, including wages paid to employees. For some very simple businesses (like a newspaper dealer who rents a kiosk, buys newspapers every day for 10 cents and sells them for a quarter), business profits would be the same under the existing income tax and the Disguised Invisible Flat Tax. But if our friendly newspaper dealer decided to buy his own kiosk, purchase a truck to make deliveries to other dealers, buy an IBM personal computer to keep business records, or use his profits to invest in a completely different business, his taxes would drop.

Under the Disguised Invisible Flat Tax, our newspaper dealer could deduct immediately from his business profits the full amount of his business investments. As long as the business was expanding and investing its profits, he would pay no taxes at all. This favorable tax treatment of capital investment is identical to the treatment of capital expenditures under the most common form of value added tax. But this VAT is cleverly disguised to look more like the current income tax.

Under a normal, 19 percent value added tax, our friendly newspaper dealer would pay a flat 19 percent tax on his gross receipts, after subtracting all amounts paid to other businesses, such as rent and the 10 cents paid to the newspaper publisher for each daily paper. No deduction would be allowed for wages and salaries paid to any of his assistants, since those wages reflect an important part of the "value added" by the newspaper dealer in his business.

The Disguised Invisible Flat Tax allows the newspaper dealer to *subtract* the wages he pays to his assistants. But it then imposes a flat 19 percent wage tax on the assistants' salaries. The net result is a value-added tax that looks more like an income tax because it is divided into a business tax and a wage tax. But if you collapse the two taxes, it's almost identical to a VAT. The key difference is that modest exemptions to the wage tax are allowed, similar to the current exemptions and standard deductions under the income tax.

The Wage Tax

The second part of the Disguised Invisible Flat Tax would impose a flat 19 percent tax on all cash wages paid to employees, above a minimum exempt amount. A married couple with two children could claim a marital exemption of $6,700 and two dependency exemptions worth $810 for each child. (The total exempt amount of $8,320 is almost the same as the current income tax threshold of $8,783. Both figures are about $2,000 below the official poverty level of $10,613.) The flat tax on cash wages would be the only income tax paid by individuals, and it would be withheld by employers just like the current income tax. The social security payroll tax of 7 percent paid by the employer and 7 percent paid by the employee would remain.

Under this new wage tax, the typical family of four receiving $26,000 in wage income would pay $3,360 in wage taxes. In contrast, under the current income tax, with no special deductions they would pay only $2,899 in income taxes, so their income tax bill would be increased by almost $500! (That is part of the reason this tax plan can afford to be so generous to investors and businesses.)

What about higher income families? It's difficult to say precisely how much their taxes would be affected by the Disguised Invisible Flat Tax because the most important thing about this flat wage tax is that *there are no deductions. Period.* For many families, that would mean a tax increase. But there would certainly be individual cases where taxpayers would benefit from a substantial tax reduction or experience a sharp tax increase. That's because the second most important thing about this tax is that income from savings and investments are *not subject to the wage tax.*

Because this flat wage tax allows no deductions and completely exempts savings and investment income, the changes in individual tax burdens can be quite dramatic. A family earning $45,000 in salary income that claimed the standard deduction under current law would experience a tax reduction of about $1,200. But a family that had just purchased a home and was deducting $12,000 in mortgage interest and property taxes would have a whopping tax increase of around $1,400! And anyone who was living off interest on the savings accumulated during a lifetime of hard work (or inherited from the accumulation of someone else's lifetime of hard work) would suddenly be in the enviable position of paying no individual income taxes. Period.

It's pretty obvious that one of the biggest problems with the Disguised Invisible Flat Tax, as well as many other proposals for major reform, is the transition from the real world of today, to the "ideal" tax system of tomorrow. Even if Congress did agree on a system for the future, there would be problems "getting there from here."

Why Is This Tax So Generous to Business and Investment?

The favorable treatment accorded to capital investment by the Disguised Invisible Flat Tax goes beyond simply deferring taxes when a business is growing and investing its profits. The individual owners of a business pay no taxes on the distribution of the firm's profits, and investors who lend money to the business pay no taxes on their interest income. The theory of this approach is that the income generated from investing in the stock or debt of a business is subject to tax once, at the business level. There is no need to tax the income again (supporters argue) when it is earned by a stockholder or bondholder.

And, because the treatment of capital expenditures is based simply on the cash flow of the business, there is no need for complex depreciation provisions. Because the income from savings and investment is taxed once, at a flat 19 percent rate, there are no complex provisions designed to measure long-term and short-term capital gains and no special tax-favored forms of investment like low-income housing or oil drilling.

The result is a tax law that is eight pages long and tax forms that can fit on the back of a postcard.

Transitional Problems: Is Simplification Worth It?

Substitution of a Disguised Invisible Flat Tax for the complete individual and corporate income tax would create serious transition problems for many individuals who have made investments relying on the income tax rules currently in force. Mortgage interest deductions, for example, would not be permitted. The authors of this tax reform proposal believe that mortgage interest rates would decline because of the fact that interest income would be tax-exempt. But even if that did occur, many homeowners would need to refinance their mortgages, and the disruptions to the market for single-family residences could be substantial.

Another "transition" problem with any new tax on consumer spending—whether it is visible, invisible, or disguised—is the impact on individuals who have been paying income taxes and saving money without any inkling that a national sales tax might one day be adopted. A nest egg of $1,000 would suddenly have only $910 of purchasing power if a 10 percent sales tax or VAT were imposed tomorrow.

BEING HONEST WITH OURSELVES ABOUT TAXING SAVINGS

An immediate transition from the current income tax system to a flat tax on consumer spending—whether it is in the form of the "One Day at a Time" Flat Tax, the Invisible Flat Tax, or the Disguised Invisible Flat Tax—is unlikely. But the possibility of a gradual transition from taxing income to taxing consumption is a real possibility. The strongest argument in favor of such a transition is the fact that the existing income tax is already filled with special exemptions and preferences for many types of investment income. Tax-exempt municipal bonds are, as their name implies, free of tax on the interest income paid to the bondholder, even if he or she is a multimillionaire. Real estate investments generally enjoy what's called a "negative tax rate." That means that the special deductions are so generous, they not only wipe out any tax on the rental income, but they are an investment commonly used to "shelter" other unrelated income from federal income taxes. And the corporate tax burden is not shared evenly by different types of businesses. The statutory corporate tax rate is 46 percent, but the average amount of taxes actually paid is less than 30 percent.

Tax experts agree that the effective tax rates of different industries vary widely (depending in part on how successful their Washington lobbyists have been). In 1983, the Congressional Joint Committee on Taxation found that the effective tax rates of the largest corporations in America varied from less than one percent all the way up to 35.6 percent, depending on the industry. The same sort of imbalances can be found in the individual income tax, depending on the extent to which tax-sheltered investments are taken advantage of.

If a tax increase is necessary, these inequities would only be magnified by proposals to simply raise the statutory tax rates, or to impose what's called a "surcharge"—an added tax equal to a flat percentage of the taxes already due. If the income tax isn't going to be scrapped tomorrow for a tax on consumption—as some reformers think should be done—there's another group of reformers ready with their plans for "A New and Improved" Income Tax.

4

An Imaginary Cocktail Party Conversation (in Two Acts)

INTRODUCTION

The chapter after this one describes some of the major proposals designed to develop a "new and improved" income tax instead of scrapping it for a tax on consumption. Most of them sound like they belong in a health club or Nautilus Center, since they talk a lot about "base broadening" and "rate flattening." As far as we know, there are no paperback books in the supermarket with pictures of senators in leotards telling you "How to Flatten Your Rates and Develop a Broader Tax Base In 30 Days."

That's because what they mean when they talk about "base broadening" is making sure that all kinds of income are subject to tax—like interest on municipal bonds, which is now completely exempt from the federal income tax, and long-term capital gains on stocks, which are slightly more than half-exempt. "Rate flattening" means lowering the tax rates for higher income families (or raising the tax rates for lower income families) so that lower and higher income families pay closer to an equal proportion of their incomes in taxes. Come to think of it, "base broadening" and "rate flattening" aren't really that different from what goes on at a typical fitness club. Very few of our senators and congressmen seem to want a *completely* flat tax rate or a *totally* comprehensive tax base. But having the curves, valleys, and bumps in just the "right" places can make all the difference in the world.

Virtually all cash wages and salaries are completely included in the income tax base—the only exception is an exclusion for the first $80,000 of income earned by Americans working in foreign countries. So the question of how broad the tax base should be is pretty much a question of how much income from savings and investment should be taxed. Broadening the tax base to include all kinds of income from savings and investment is the exact opposite of what the consumption taxes discussed in the last chapter would do.

We've already seen that taxing savings and investment income raises difficult issues of fairness. Our friend Jim Johnson in Chapter 2 (who saved $2,000 from his $20,000 salary) thinks it's unfair "double taxation" to tax the $200 of interest income he earned from putting his savings in a money market fund. But he's not wild about the idea of letting Biff and Tad Phillips escape taxes on the $200,000 a year they each receive in dividends from their stock in the Phillips Construction Company. Aside from the issue of fairness, there are serious questions being asked about whether a comprehensive tax on savings and investment income will discourage the savings and investment that are needed to keep the economy strong.

Flattening the tax rates is also a double-edged issue. On the one hand, there are obvious questions of whether fairness demands (or permits!) a system where wealthier people not only pay "more," but pay "much more" as a percentage of their annual income. On the other hand, regardless of what "fairness demands," some people believe that high tax rates will discourage work and savings and the kind of risky investments that often return as much to the society as a whole as they do to the lucky or skillful entrepreneur. Fairness is a very personal issue that unfortunately doesn't have any hard and fast answers. We know it doesn't mean treating everyone the same, or else we would adopt the simple "I Didn't Mean *That* Flat" Tax. But it also doesn't mean letting illegal drug dealers pay nothing, while retail pharmacists pay an effective corporate tax rate of 20 percent.

What about the economic arguments against high tax rates? And the ongoing debate about whether our tax system should encourage more work, savings, and investment? Let's try to divorce those questions from the fairness issue, and take a tough, hardnosed look at them. Not from the perspective of pointy-headed economists who "never had to meet a payroll," but from the no-nonsense perspective of the real world.

Well, almost real. Let's listen in to a series of imaginary cocktail party conversations about work, savings and investment, and the tax system.

AN IMAGINARY COCKTAIL PARTY CONVERSATION: ACT ONE

It is dusk in late August of 1980. The scene is a penthouse apartment in New York City, overlooking Central Park. William E. Bentley (chairman of the multi-million-dollar Bentley Corporation) and Mrs. Edith Bentley, are hosting a fund-raising cocktail party for the Reagan-Bush election campaign.

Standing next to a grand piano, near a picture window looking south toward Wall Street are William Bentley and one of his guests, Bob Marino. Marino is the successful boss of Marino Advertising, the agency that handles the Bentley account.

Bentley: I'm pleased you could make it, Bob. I feel this campaign is important, very important for companies like ours.

Marino: You know I wouldn't *willingly* miss one of your parties, Bill. And I agree about the election. Jimmy Carter is a *disaster*.

Bentley: Oh, but there's so much more than just that, Bob. Reagan's really got the right ideas to get the economy back on track. The most important thing is to get these tax rates down so we'll all have more incentives to work, save, and invest.

Marino: Taxes *are* incredible, Bill. I'll drink to that. (raises glass, sips) But I didn't actually *major* in economics. . . How do they figure a tax cut will increase work and productivity?

Bentley: It's rather simple, Bob. You know we all work hard for the money we earn and we don't even get to keep 50 cents on the dollar. The IRS takes half, and then there's state income tax and the god damned city taxes. Most of our employees aren't in the top tax brackets, but they also have to pay social security taxes. It's no wonder the incentives to work hard aren't what they used to be. With lower tax rates all of us will keep more of our incomes. The incentives will be greater and Americans will work harder, and work smarter, to earn that extra dollar.

Marino: Hmm . . . . I see.

Bentley: You don't sound convinced. Let me try to bring it home. You own your own business, 100 percent. Every dollar you earn is yours, after taxes of course. If you had a partner, you'd only keep half of every dollar the firm earned. Well, a 50 percent tax rate is like having the government as your silent partner. I'm sure you work harder and care more when the profits are all yours, than when you share them. Convinced yet?

Marino: Well, yes and no.

Bentley: All right, Bob. You know I respect your judgment. What makes you skeptical?

Marino: I used to be in a partnership with three other guys, and you're absolutely right, I care more and work harder now that I'm on my own. But our business, the advertising industry, is based on kind of a funny view of human nature. We start from the point of view that a guy or gal making $40,000 or $50,000—or even less—can afford just about *everything* they *really* need. You know, food, clothing, and shelter. If he doesn't love his job—he doesn't really have any incentive to work any harder just to afford the bare necessities, or even to be reasonably comfortable. That's where we come in.

A lot of the ads we write are designed to make people who have what they really need believe that they need more. You know—a more expensive car, a $2,000 wristwatch, a bigger and better home. It's become so much a part of American life, most folks don't even realize how they get manipulated by snob appeal. And it works. Most of us are hooked on constantly making more and spending more as a way of life. It's the American dream I guess. Or the American nightmare maybe.

Bentley: Then you agree with me?

Marino: Well, not exactly. If most Americans are hooked on spending more each year, then they don't really have much of a choice. If taxes are high, and the government is taking 50 cents on the dollar, then we'll have to work twice as hard to get that extra dollar just so we can spend 50 cents. The only real choice the average guy or gal has is between working for whatever is left after taxes or not working and *not* taking home even half of what he *could* earn. Of course, there are some people who would rather sit in the backyard with a can of beer all weekend than work Saturdays just so they can afford to drink Chivas Regal when they get home.

Bentley: Well, then, you agree that high tax rates discourage work and encourage leisure!

Marino: Yes. But if we're doing our job of brainwashing the American consumer to want Chivas Regal, then the tax rates would have to be extremely high to really discourage work and encourage leisure. And for the people who are spending money just so other people know they're spending it, I'm not sure they'd be discouraged much before the tax rate reached 99 percent.

Bentley: Now I'm not sure I follow you.

Marino: Well, I guess what I'm saying is if people make money in order to spend it, and they have something *specific* in mind to spend it on, raising the tax rates will only make them work harder to get it. I suppose if they can make something for themselves— like distilling their own bathtub gin or bottling their own wine— then Beefeaters and Gallo might lose some sales.

Bentley: And that would hurt the economy!

Marino: Sure, Bill, but I just don't know whether a 50 percent, 70 percent, or even a 90 percent tax rate is going to turn our country into a nation of do-it-yourselfers. Especially the higher income, up-scale folks, who are suckers for the ads we write for Chivas Regal, Johnny Walker Black Label, and Rolex.

(Enter from stage left, Mrs. Edith Bentley.)

Edith: Let me freshen your drink, Bob. What's your pleasure?

Marino: Oh, just another Perrier water. Thanks, Edith.

(Edith walks over to a bar cart near the piano, pours a small bottle of Perrier water into a 6-ounce glass, adds three ice cubes and a twist of lime. Hands glass to Bob Marino.)

Bentley: Edith, you're just in time to settle our debate on whether high tax rates discourage work . . . .

Marino: . . . Or *encourage* work.

Edith: Well, I overheard a bit of what you boys were saying, and I think you've both missed the boat. I agree with Bob that high tax rates won't discourage a *rational* person who's hooked on spending money from working. But both of you have forgotten about the emotional factor.

Marino: You mean envy? The driving force of our economy?

Edith: No. I mean *spite*—the willingness to hurt yourself just to hurt someone else you resent.

Bentley: How does that affect the equation, dear?

Edith: When the tax rates are seen as too high—confiscatory, in other words—then people will go to great lengths to hire tax lawyers and accountants, invest in fly-by-night tax shelters, and even cheat on their taxes because there's so much to be gained from hiding a dollar of income. At a 70 percent tax rate, a dollar's worth of productive work will only bring me 30 cents of purchasing power. But if I can figure out a way of hiding or sheltering a dollar of income, I will have 70 cents more in my pocketbook without adding anything productive to the society. Even if I only postpone taxation for a few years I can invest that 70 cents and earn 7 cents in interest each year! Lowering the tax rates may or may not increase work. But it seems to me it would *have* to reduce tax cheating and investments in nonproductive tax shelters.

Marino: I don't know, Edie, I agree with you as a matter of theory, but some habits are hard to break.

Bentley: Well, let's all drink to the Reagan-Bush team. If we're lucky, we'll have a real-live laboratory experiment, and we can discuss the results four years from now when we're gathering for a *re*-election bash!

(They all smile, touch glasses, take a sip of their drinks, and begin discussing the stock market.)

AN IMAGINARY COCKTAIL PARTY CONVERSATION: ACT TWO

The scene is the summer home of Bob Marino and his wife, Peggy, in East Hampton, Long Island. The Marino's and their weekend guests, the Bentley's, are relaxing on the porch with cool, tall drinks after three sets of strenuous mixed doubles. It is August 25, 1984, a few days after the close of the Republican National Convention in Dallas.

Edith: This place is absolutely marvelous, Peggy. How long have you and Bob had it?

Peggy: Oh, we bought it in the spring of 1982.

Marino: Yeah, and we practically stole the place. I was having a good year. I'd gotten out of the stock market just in time—before the bottom fell out in the summer of 1981. With high interest rates and the recession and all, it was a real buyer's market, especially for anyone with cash.

Bentley: Those were two smart moves, Bob. Very smart.

Marino: Thanks, Bill. But you know I don't know what to do now. The economy seems terrific, and the market's been up for a few weeks, but it's hard to see what's coming.

Bentley: Well you can thank the president for how well the economy's going. And if he's re-elected, I think the stock market will soar.

Marino: What about the deficit, Bill? Are they going to raise taxes like Mondale says?

Bentley: I suppose they may have to, as a last resort.

Bob: I remember our discussion about high taxes and work. Do you think any of us was proved right?

Bentley: Despite the economic boom, I won't claim to be proved right. The tax changes were frankly overshadowed by the Federal Reserve Board's tight money policy. How else can you explain a depression in 1982 after the biggest tax cut in history?

Edith: I'll admit to being dead wrong. We heard about more tax shelters than ever, even with a reduction of the maximum tax rate from 70 percent to 50 percent.

Bentley: Well, to be fair to you, Edie, we were all talking about a straight rate reduction. You had no idea Congress was also going to make existing tax shelters much more lucrative by increasing depreciation deductions. What they did was not only flatten the tax rates, they also narrowed the tax base. Of course, the 1982 and 1984 tax bills reversed that somewhat.

Peggy: Well, what do you think will happen next year, Bill, with all the talk about deficits and taxes?

Bentley: A lot depends on the election, of course. But whoever is in office, the most important thing is not *whether* they raise taxes, but *how* they raise taxes.

Marino: What do you mean?

Bentley: Well, Bob, the problem with our tax system is that it discourages saving and investment. We need more tax incentives for capital formation to be more competitive in the international marketplace.

Peggy: You mean like the Individual Retirement Account?

Bentley: Well, that's the idea, but the IRA doesn't go far enough. We should be moving away completely from an income tax and adopt some form of a tax on consumption. It's the only way to increase the amount of saving and investment in the private sector.

Marino: How would that work, Bill?

Bentley: Well, there are a number of ways it could be done—a sales tax, a value-added tax, or even just excluding savings from the tax base until the money was spent.

Edith: That would be a powerful incentive to save and not to spend. You know, it's not surprising that Americans spend too much and save too little. You give up something to put a little away in a bank account, and the next thing you know, you have to pay taxes on the interest. That's double taxation!

Peggy: Well, I'm not sure I agree. People may gripe about taxes, but I don't think there would be any more saving if we didn't have to pay taxes on interest and dividends.

Bentley: What makes you say that Peggy?

Peggy: Well, you know, I'm a stockbroker, and advising people on their finances is my business. I find that people who save and invest money basically come in two types. There are the customers who are saving with a particular goal in mind, like paying for their children's education, buying a business or a home—you name it. Then there are the customers who just feel deep down that they're spending enough, or more than enough, and should be putting some money away. Either they want it for the proverbial rainy day or they would just feel guilty if they didn't save money.

Bentley: Well, wouldn't they save more if the tax system didn't discourage them?

Peggy: Not necessarily. The customers with the goal in mind might actually save less, since without any taxes on interest or dividends they'd reach their goal faster.

Edith: And what about your other customers?

Peggy: Well, if they're spending all they really want—and truly want to

save and invest the rest—then taxes shouldn't make any difference. If they really want to save, they have no real choice,
regardless of the rate of taxation on investment.

Bentley: You don't think replacing the income tax with a sales tax or
value-added tax would encourage more saving and capital
formation?

Peggy: Not for my customers, Bill.

Marino: Well, you know, maybe Peggy's customers are all perfectly
rational creatures. But I think there's an irrational element at
work here. I hate to say it but I think it operates in favor of Bill's
argument for a tax on spending.

Edith: Why do you hate to say it, Bob?

Marino: Well, increased saving is really just another way of saying that
consumers are *spending* less. And that can't be good for my
advertising business.

Peggy: Okay, but what's this irrational element you're talking about,
honey?

Marino: Well, as I see it, what you want to do here is change people's
attitudes and behavior. And we're talking fundamental attitudes. I mean, 50 years ago the big achievement was to pay *off*
the mortgage. Now, the bigger the mortgage the better. Borrowing is good, and paying cash is bad.

Bentley: That's because of the tax deduction for mortgage interest.

Marino: Well, sure, that makes it easier. But that deduction has been
around for decades. The change in attitudes has taken a long
time. It's probably been fueled by inflation more than the tax
laws. And what about consumer borrowing? Twenty years
ago borrowing money to take a vacation was almost immoral.
Today, with the "me" generation, it's almost a sin to deny
yourself anything that a little borrowed money can buy.
Those attitudes changed dramatically over the last few gen-
erations and it's going to be difficult to change them back.

Peggy: So how does that relate to tax incentives for saving?

Marino: Well, in order to change basic attitudes you have to do something dramatic. I'll agree that a rational person shouldn't
change his behavior just because consumption is taxed or
saving is tax-free. But a tax change could really provide a daily
shot of reinforcement for all the rhetoric about saving for our
country's future. That's especially true of a sales tax. Every

time you went to purchase something, you would know that you were also paying taxes, and if you deferred the purchase, you'd defer the taxes.

Edith: I agree, Bob. And if income taxes didn't have to be paid on income that was saved, we'd get a little pat on the back when we deferred a purchase, instead of the slap in the face of having to pay taxes a second time!

Peggy: But, honey, I don't understand. With a sales tax you either pay it now, or you pay it later when you finally break down and buy something. And with an income tax that exempted savings until they were withdrawn from an account and actually spent, you'll pay the tax eventually. It shouldn't make any difference, really!

Marino: I agree it *shouldn't*. But I believe it would. We're all basically a little nearsighted about money. We have to be trained to be prudent—and every near-term psychological reward helps— like seeing your quarterly bank statement or getting a dividend check.

Bentley: There I agree with you, Bob. There's no rational reason many investors should want dividends on common stock, especially since dividends are taxed more heavily than capital gains on the sale of stock. But a healthy annual dividend sort of assures them that the company is sound.

Peggy: Let me get this straight, Bob. You're agreeing with me that an educated consumer and a rational investor wouldn't be affected by changes in the taxation of savings and spending. But the tax law could be used to provide purely psychological rewards for saving and punishments for spending.

Marino: You've got it. Of course, I'd prefer that they didn't change anything. Except maybe hire our firm for a series of television spots to encourage investing in America's future. We can use the business.

Bentley: I'll second that motion, Bob. (They all laugh.)

Peggy: Well, anyone for a game of Trivial Pursuit?

(They all express enthusiasm, and as Peggy sets up the game, the curtain falls.)

5

A "New and Improved" Income Tax?

Even without a tax increase, the federal income tax is not going to win any popularity contests. Despite the widely held view of the "tax experts" that a tax on income with graduated rates is the fairest way to raise needed revenue, less than half of the American people believe the income tax is "fair," and many believe it is the "worst tax" Americans pay—even less "fair" than sales taxes which the "experts" say are the most regressive taxes paid by the average citizen.

If taxes are to be increased, any proposal that just raises existing tax rates or imposes a simple "surcharge" (an added tax equal to a percentage of everyone's existing income tax bill) would only magnify the existing problems. If you're not paying any income taxes now, a "surcharge" is the perfect way to raise taxes, since your immunity from taxation would be preserved.

"Soaking the rich" and making big corporations pay more are slogans more than strategies (Chapter 8 has some guidance on how to turn them into strategies.) And their value even as slogans is questionable, now that many liberals admit that individual tax rates are too high and "Atari Democrats" say that American business needs a climate more conducive to increased saving and investment.

The existing progressive income tax is over 70 years old. The basic income tax code was adopted over 30 years ago, in 1954. During the last 15 years it has been "reformed" three times (1969, 1976, and 1984) and substantially amended almost every other year. No one has quite yet come out and said "You can't trust a tax code over 30." But that may be because Jerry Rubin is working on Wall Street.

A simple, flat tax on consumer spending is one of the available options for "fundamental" reform. But it is unlikely that a "One Day at a Time" Flat Tax (national sales tax) or an Invisible Flat Tax (value-added tax) will completely replace the individual or corporate income tax right away. The adoption of a national tax based on consumption could begin a gradual, counterrevolutionary tax reform that might lead to the "withering away" of the income tax as we know it. (Just as a modest income tax affecting less than one percent of the population in 1913 grew 100 times faster than the population and replaced tariffs and consumption taxes as the workhorse of the federal tax system.)

Meaningful reform is the enemy of revolution. And each member of the new generation of reformers believes he or she has developed a New and Improved Income Tax that is both more simple (it won't leave your accountant with dish-pan hands) and more fair (it won't upset your stomach). Before we go for a test drive, let's take one more close look at the "lemon" we're thinking of trading in. Readers who are familiar with the existing income tax and want to skip ahead should do so. But be sure to glance at the tables on pages 119 and 108, illustrating the way the corporate income tax burden is shared and the amount of actual progressivity of the individual income tax.

A SNAPSHOT VIEW OF THE FEDERAL INCOME TAX

The progressive income tax and the flat social security payroll tax on wages dwarf all other sources of revenue currently used by the federal government. Close to $670 billion was raised in 1984, and more than $600 billion of that came from income and payroll taxes. (Of course, in addition to using all of that, the government spent another $180 billion or so of borrowed money.)

About $355 billion in revenue came from individual and corporate income taxes. About half again as much would have been needed to balance the budget, which explains why a simple tax increase without spending cuts is unlikely to be very attractive. An across-the-board, 50 percent increase in federal income taxes is almost unimaginable.

CORPORATE TAXES

The income tax on corporations is imposed at a 46 percent rate, theoretically making the federal government a silent partner sharing almost half of all corporate profits. In fact, the average tax rate of corporate America is closer to 30 percent, with some industries paying less than 10 percent and others paying more than 40 percent.

Generous allowances for capital investment is the most significant single factor responsible for reducing corporate tax receipts and for the widely varying tax burdens of different industries. In 1984, the corporate income tax raised about $60 billion. But an estimated $34 billion more was *not* collected because of the "tax expenditures" attributable to the investment tax credit and accelerated cost recovery allowances for capital investments.

Corporate profits are taxed once by the corporate income tax, and once again when the after-tax profits are distributed to shareholders in the form of dividends. But the sale of corporate stock or the liquidation of a corporation are methods available to get cash profits out of a corporation and into the hands of an individual without declaring a taxable dividend. Sales and liquidations are generally taxed as "long term" capital gains, which takes some of the sting out of the "double taxation" of corporate profits. That is because long-term capital gains are only partially taxable to individuals.

INDIVIDUAL TAXES

Individuals pay income taxes on wages and salaries, interest and corporate dividends, rents and royalties, and income from businesses that are operated either as a sole proprietorship or partnership (and not subject to the corporate income tax). Profits from the purchase and sale of corporate stock, land, gold coins, apartment buildings, and other investments are taxed as capital gains. If the stock or property is held for at least 6 months, only 40 percent of the gain is taxable. In addition, no taxes are paid on "paper profits" until the stock or property is actually sold or exchanged (unlike interest on a bond, rent from an apartment building, or royalties from an oil well, which are generally taxed every year when they are received).

The individual income tax is levied at marginal rates ranging from 11 percent to 50 percent. The tax is predominantly a tax on wages and salaries. More than 80 percent of the income reported on returns filed in 1981 was from wages and salaries. The next largest source of income was interest, accounting for less than 8 percent.

An even smaller amount was attributable to capital gains on the sale of corporate stock and property. Almost $80 billion in capital gains were reported by individuals. After applying the special rules for taxing capital gains and losses, only $31 billion was fully subject to tax, less than 2 percent of the income reported by individuals.

Capital gains and corporate dividends are generally a more significant source of income for wealthier Americans. Even so, wages and salaries account for more than half of the individual income reported on the vast majority of tax returns, even for individuals earning as much as $200,000.

There were about 175,000 Americans reporting income greater than $200,000 for 1981. For these wealthy few (less than one-fifth of one percent of income tax return filers and an even smaller fraction of the the general population) average income was almost half a million dollars. For the "average" taxpayer of this very unaverage group, 30 percent of income was derived from salary, 20 percent from interest and dividends, and more than 40 percent from capital gains (although only about 40 percent of this 40 percent was subject to tax).

The Progressive Rate Structure

The individual income tax has a "graduated" or "progressive" rate schedule, designed to ensure that wealthier people not only pay "more" but pay "much more" as a percentage of their annual incomes. But the gradually increasing tax rates or "tax brackets" apply only to the additional amounts earned at the margin. For example, a married couple reporting $200,000 will pay a 50 percent tax rate only on the amount of income that exceeds $162,400, the lower boundary of the so-called 50 percent tax bracket. Amounts between $109,400 and $162,400 are taxed at 49 percent, amounts between $85,600 and $109,400 are taxed at 45 percent, and so on down to the lowest bracket where income under $3,400 is not subject to any tax.

This series of marginal tax brackets is used to avoid the situation where earning an additional dollar of income would cost more than a dollar in taxes. Under the system of gradually increasing marginal tax rates, only the additional "marginal" dollar is taxed at a higher marginal tax rate. As a result, even a married couple in the 50 percent bracket will receive the benefit of lower marginal rates on their first $162,400 of taxable income (and thus should approach, but never actually pay 50 percent of their income in taxes). The following table illustrates the actual amount of tax due, as a percentage of taxable income, at various income levels because of this system of increasing marginal rate brackets. The calculations assume a married couple filing jointly.

Taxable income	Income tax	Tax as Percentage of Income
$ 20,000	$ 1,741	8.7
$ 50,000	$ 9,848	19.7
$100,000	$ 32,400	32.4
$200,000	$ 81,400	40.7
$500,000	$231,400	46.3

But *taxable* income is not the same as real *economic* income. As a result, the tax system is far less "progressive" than this table might indicate. Because of the rules permitting itemized deductions for home mortgage interest, state and local taxes, charitable contributions, medical costs, and certain other expenses, not all income is fully subject to these tax rates. In addition, investment income is subject to a variety of favorable rules ranging from complete tax exemption on municipal bond interest and the partial exclusion of long-term capital gains, to complex cost recovery rules for investments in everything from apartment buildings to oil wells.

The net result is a distribution of tax burdens that is far less "progressive" than the marginal rate tables would imply, but probably more "progressive" than most people believe to be the case. Precise estimates of the real economic income of individual taxpayers are difficult to obtain from examining tax returns because, among other problems, billions of dollars of interest on municipal bonds held by individuals are not even reported on tax forms. But Treasury Department estimates based on information disclosed on individual tax returns and computer simulations reveal that the individual income tax does require higher income families to pay "much more" as a percentage of real economic income.

Who Gains from Flat Taxes?

One approximate measure of economic income, called "expanded income," has been used by the IRS and the Congressional Joint Committee on Taxation to measure the progressivity of the income tax. Using this concept, families with incomes below $10,000 pay less than 4 percent, middle income families with incomes between $20,000 and $30,000 pay about 11 percent, higher income families earning between $50,000 and $100,000 pay almost 17 percent, and the richest families earning more than $200,000 pay almost 25 percent.

The Treasury Department has developed a more comprehensive definition of "economic income." According to the Treasury Department's most recent estimates, families with economic incomes below $10,000 pay less than 2 percent of their incomes in income taxes. Middle-income families with incomes between $20,000 and $30,000 pay about 6.2 percent of their incomes in taxes. Higher income families with incomes between $50,000 and $100,000 pay about 9.4 percent, and the highest income families earning more than $200,000 pay about 21 percent in federal income taxes.

These statistics vary sharply with the predominant public perception of the distribution of income tax burdens. They explain why a truly flat tax on all income, with no deductions and no exclusions, would lighten the income tax burden on higher income families and add to the tax burden of lower and middle income families.

A flat 20 percent tax rate on all income with no special deductions or exclusions would almost certainly provide a tax cut for most of the estimated 1.5 million households earning more than $75,000 each year and a tax increase for nearly everyone else. Nevertheless, numerous bills to replace the existing individual income tax with a "really flat, true income" tax have been introduced in the last four sessions of Congress.

These bills are probably more indicative of a "real" lack of public confidence in the existing system and a "true" lack of understanding of the actual distribution of income tax burdens than they are of a genuine desire to relieve the tax burden of the wealthy at the expense of the middle class.

Indeed, the more attention any particular proposal receives the more it tends to deviate from "real flatness" and "true breadth." Senator Dan Quayle of Indiana introduced the SELF Tax Plan in 1983, with moderately progressive rates ranging from 14 percent to 28 percent, and no deductions for mortgage interest, charitable contributions, medical expenses, or contributions to Individual Retirement Accounts. But the 1985 version of Senator Quayle's SELF Tax Plan (the acronym stands for *S*implicity, *E*fficiency, *L*ow tax rates, and *F*airness) would allow for all of these popular deductions and make up for the narrower tax base with slightly higher rates ranging from 15 percent to 30 percent.

THE BRADLEY-GEPHARDT FAIR TAX: WHAT YOU SEE IS NOT (NECESSARILY) WHAT YOU'LL GET

Senator Bill Bradley of New Jersey and Missouri Congressman Dick Gephardt, authors of the so-called "FAIR Tax Act," avoided at least two of the pitfalls encountered by some other tax reform measures. For one thing, "FAIR" is not an acronym—the letters don't stand for anything other than the sponsors' belief that their bill would produce a fair tax system.

Bradley and Gephardt and the other mostly Democratic supporters of the plan say it is "fair" because it would not shift the tax burden from high-income taxpayers to low- and moderate-income taxpayers as would the purely flat tax reform proposals. The FAIR Tax Act also wouldn't change the amount of taxes paid by corporations as compared with individuals. Instead, the Bradley-Gephardt tax plan would preserve the existing distribution of individual and corporate tax burdens by lowering the statutory tax rates and bringing more excluded items into the tax base.

The second pitfall avoided by the Bradley-Gephardt plan is openly treading on sacred cows, like the mortgage interest deduction. The sponsors admit to facing up to political realities in crafting a tax reform bill that, in Senator Bradley's words, keeps those special tax provisions "that are most beneficial to middle-income people such as the deductions for home mortgage interest, charitable contributions, state and local income and property taxes, and some medical and business expenses . . . exclusions for veterans' benefits and social security benefits and the exemption for interest on general obligation (municipal bonds), IRAs, and Keoghs." But, in Senator Bradley's words, "The rest of the tax preferences we pretty much eliminate."

The FAIR tax plan was years in the making, with the first half of the bill affecting individuals unveiled in the summer of 1982 and the second half addressing corporate taxation introduced on June 8, 1983. But with the Bradley-Gephardt FAIR Tax, what you see is not necessarily what you'll get.

How the FAIR Tax Treats Moderate-Income Taxpayers

On its face, the FAIR tax plan is rather simple for the majority of individual taxpayers. The maximum tax rate is reduced from 50 percent to 30 percent and all taxpayers are placed in one of only three tax brackets.

About 80 percent of existing taxpayers (married couples earning less than $40,000 and individuals earning less than $25,000) would be in the bottom tax bracket, where income will be taxed at a flat 14 percent rate. A standard deduction of $3,000 for an individual and $6,000 for a married couple would be allowed. Additional exemptions of $1,600 for each taxpayer and $1,000 for each dependent would also be allowed. These exempt amounts are somewhat more generous than existing law and were designed to ensure that families below the official federal poverty level pay no income tax.

For taxpayers in the bottom 14 percent bracket, the most popular deductions will be completely unaffected, including the deduction for home mortgage interest and real property taxes, state and local income taxes, charitable contributions, major medical expenses, and the deduction for contributions to IRA and KEOGH plans. But the deduction for state and local sales taxes will be eliminated, which should provide an incentive for state and local governments to shift completely from sales taxes to income or property taxes. (This discrimination is difficult to justify on grounds of simplification and amounts to a federal incentive for states to rely more heavily on taxes viewed by the "tax experts" as more "fair.")

The majority of taxpayers in the 14 percent tax bracket will not be directly affected by Bradley-Gephardt's changes in the taxation of individual investment income—most notably the elimination of the $100 dividend exclusion, the end to favorable treatment for long-term capital gains, and restrictions on certain types of municipal bonds. But a number of "fringe benefits" enjoyed by many wage earners would become taxable—including group term life insurance, child care, educational assistance, group legal services, and most important, health insurance premiums paid by employers.

If these fringe benefits are not eliminated, individual tax returns would be required to include the cash value of the fringe benefits provided. Unemployment compensation would also be fully taxable.

For families with children, the child care credit would be replaced with a deduction, and the deduction for adoption expenses would be repealed. The special deduction for two-earner couples designed to reduce the "marriage penalty" tax would also be eliminated, supposedly because the flat tax rate on a married couple's income below $40,000 reduces the need for the provision.

Indexing of tax brackets for inflation is also eliminated on the basis of a similar assertion that the lower, flatter tax rates makes the problem of bracket creep less serious. And, apparently for the same reason, income averaging for individuals with sharply fluctuating incomes is also repealed.

So far, the tax law is not much different for taxpayers in this 14 percent tax bracket. Life will not be very much simpler either, since nearly all of the widely used deductions are retained, and the vast majority of this group doesn't itemize deductions in any event.

The FAIR Tax and the Fortunate Minority

But beyond the upper boundary of the 14 percent tax bracket ($40,000 for a married couple and $25,000 for an individual) more than 15 million households will be banished from this safe, familiar world preserved for the majority. These upper-income taxpayers will now have to compute two completely different income taxes. First, they will pay a flat 14 percent tax on their taxable incomes, computed just like their friends in the 14 percent tax bracket. Then, they will have to compute what's called a "surtax," an added tax of 12 percent in the middle-bracket and 16 percent for the top-bracket families. On the surface, this seems to say that you pay 14 percent in the first bracket, 26 percent in the second bracket, and 30 percent in the top bracket. But watch closely!

None of the popular deductions preserved for "the majority" can be used in the top tax brackets! For an example of how it works, see the box on page 68.

Because the tax rates have been lowered, the plan's restriction of the most widely used deductions does not result in any immediate tax increase. And what you see is what you get, for now. But let's look forward a few years, and see what happens after five years of relatively

FAIR DEDUCTIONS

Let's say a married couple with two children earns $75,000, pays $7,500 in state income taxes, $2,000 in real property taxes, and is paying $15,000 in interest on a $125,000 mortgage on a newly acquired home worth $150,000. Their taxable income subject to the 14 percent tax is only $45,300. (Since they can deduct mortgage interest, income and real property taxes, and $5,200 in personal exemptions.) That results in a 14 percent flat tax of $6,342.

Now comes the fun. For a married couple the middle tax bracket applies between $40,000 and $65,000, and the top tax bracket kicks in above $65,000. But no deductions are permitted in these brackets. That means they pay an additional flat tax of 12 percent on the amount of income in the middle bracket between $40,000 and $65,000 ($25,000) and an additional flat 16 percent on the amount in the top bracket above $65,000 ($10,000). That means added taxes of $3,000 and $1,600 for a grand total of $10,942. Now, true to the sponsors' stated goals, this is about the same amount of taxes this family *currently* pays. In fact, it's a tax *reduction* of around $400. So what's the problem? Read on!

modest, 5 percent inflation. The FAIR tax repeals indexation of the tax brackets. That means that in five years, without a real increase in wages but only a cost-of-living increase, our friends making $75,000 should be earning $95,000. That $20,000 increase only represents the increased cost of living, not any increased purchasing power. But that $20,000 will be taxed at a 30 percent rate with no deductions, taking $6,000 for the government and leaving only $14,000. Instead of paying $10,942 in taxes out of a $75,000 income (14.6 percent) they will be paying $16,942 in taxes out of a $95,000 income (17.8 percent). That's tantamount to a 20 percent *real* tax increase without any legislative action. (If you have any doubts, the bill is estimated to raise $10 to $20 billion more than the current law in 1987 and 1988, primarily because of this built-in tax increase.)

A New Scourge: "Deduction Reduction"

Now, take a close look at a middle-income family earning $40,000 this year, not subject to the "surtax" for higher bracket taxpayers. If they don't own their own home and claim the $6,000 Bradley-Gephardt standard deduction they'll pay $4,116 in taxes or about 10 percent of their income. Let's assume that 5 years of modest, 5 percent inflation brings their income up to $51,000. If they were waiting to buy a home, they'd have two surprises in store. First, inflation alone will have increased their tax bill to $6,892, almost 14 percent of their earnings. (A real tax increase of around 33 percent!) Secondly, if they now want to spend a quarter of their income on mortgage interest ($12,750), the deduction will only be usable against the 14 percent tax, not against the 12 percent "surtax" imposed on their $11,000 of cost-of-living increases during the last 5 years.

In short, inflation will not only lead to the familiar problem of bracket creep, it will also reduce the value of itemized deductions for mortgage interest, taxes, medical expenses, and charitable contributions by pushing taxpayers into the higher tax brackets where these deductions simply cannot be used! Unless the Bradley-Gephardt bill miraculously cures inflation, bracket creep will be joined by a new scourge, "deduction reduction," because of the bill's repeal of indexing and its strange "surtax" structure.

If the hidden tax increases of bracket creep are later addressed by an increase in the standard deduction or personal exemption amounts (rather than a shifting of the boundaries of the 14 percent, 26 percent, and 30 percent tax brackets) the problem of deduction reduction will only be aggravated.

The Withering Away of the Mortgage Interest Deduction

The gradual "withering away" of the deduction for mortgage interest and charitable contributions may be a good thing. But it has hardly been advertised by the bill's sponsors. Bracket creep and deduction reduction are only two of the lurking problems with the FAIR Tax. The fact is, this tax, with its broader base and lower rates that stop rising at 30 percent, raises the same amount as current law. In order to raise additional revenues, these low tax rates would need to be increased. Increasing the "surtax" rates could be the most politically attractive solution since it would affect the fewest people. Higher surtax rates would accelerate the problem of deduction reduction even in the absence of inflation.

The major victims of deduction reduction would be homeowners (whose real estate values could decline), the residential real estate industry (whose business could decline), and "upper class" charitable institutions like universities, museums, and opera companies (who would suffer a reduction in the amount of charitable contributions).

Finally, any tax rate increases required by the FAIR Tax might be much more than can be anticipated even now, since Congress might adopt new spending programs to make up for the elimination of the tax subsidies repealed by the FAIR Tax.

Many tax subsidies would undoubtedly not be missed. But the virtual elimination of tax-free private medical insurance and tax-based investment incentives could play into the hands of politicians who advocate the establishment of national health insurance and the funding of a federal investment bank to develop and implement a centrally controlled national "industrial policy."

POSSIBLE UNINTENDED CONSEQUENCES

Although proposals have been advanced to limit health care costs by imposing a dollar cap on health insurance benefits, or to require employee coinsurance to keep costs low, the full taxation of medical insurance proposed by Bradley and Gephardt could actually lead to changes in the desirability of private health insurance for lower income employees, who might prefer to receive cash. A sharp decline in the number of privately insured workers (as opposed to a reduction of the generousness of the benefits provided by insurance plans) might lead to increased support for a mandatory national health plan.

The FAIR Tax doesn't hint at anything this dramatic. But while its sponsors disavow the use of the tax code to affect social policy and investment decisions—they haven't disavowed government intervention in the economy as a matter of principal.

A New Industrial Policy?

The FAIR Tax could set the stage for a drastic increase in the tax liabilities of corporations and higher income taxpayers in order to pay for the development of an "industrial policy," to be controlled by a new federal bureaucracy. Under the FAIR Tax, virtually all of the special incentives for particular types of capital investment are repealed, including the investment tax credit for equipment, accelerated cost recovery system for depreciable property, percentage depletion of oil and mining properties, and expensing of mineral exploration and intangible oil- and gas-drilling costs.

The few tax preferences enjoyed by non-heavy industries are also repealed, including deferral of foreign source income and special bad-debt reserves for financial institutions. These "base broadening" measures help to pay for a corporate tax rate that is reduced from 46 percent to 30 percent. The net effect of these changes will be an increase in the relative share of corporate taxes paid by heavy industry and a decrease in the share paid by industries that benefit less from tax expenditures, such as trucking companies, beverage companies, computer and office equipment manufacturers, food processors, drug companies, retailers, tobacco companies, and wholesale distributors.

Here, as in the individual income tax changes, the most significant aspect of the Bradley-Gephardt bill is what is likely to happen *after* it is enacted. The bill repudiates the tax code as the mechanism of choice for influencing investment decisions. It eliminates virtually all tax incentives for individual saving and investing. Both the special treatment of long-term capital gains and the $100 exclusion of corporate dividends are eliminated. IRA deductions are permitted, but only against the 14 percent tax bracket.

But the bill obviously doesn't tie the hands of future Congresses from attempting to influence investment decisions with direct or indirect subsidies. Although such industrial policies will cost money, it will be difficult in any event for populist members of Congress to resist the temptation to raise the 30 percent tax rate on corporate profits back up to 40 or 50 percent.

Many politicians are likely to prefer giving away investment subsidies on a piecemeal basis through the annual appropriations process rather than through the tax code—for the same reason that business leaders prefer the adoption of a tax incentive. Tax provisions are "permanent" incentives, until they are repealed by an Act of Congress. A national bank for industrial development, however, would require annual appropriations with all the annual benefits that would incur to the members of Congress who controlled such an entity.

The Fair Tax and Capital Gains

One investment provision of the FAIR Tax deserves special mention. The bill repeals the special tax treatment of long-term capital gains, which are now taxed at only 40 cents on the dollar, and would be fully included in taxable income under the Bradley-Gephardt bill. Since the maximum tax rate for long-term capital gains is now 20 percent (the result of applying a 50 percent tax rate to only 40 percent of the actual capital gain) and the maximum tax rate under the Bradley-Gephardt bill is 30 percent, this may seem like a relatively modest change. But two things are worth noting.

First of all, the capital gains "loophole" around the double taxation of corporate income (described on page 61) will be effectively closed. Corporate profits will be taxed once at a 30 percent rate and once again at a maximum 30 percent rate when distributed to investors—even if the company's stock is sold or liquidated. The most "progressive" view of the corporate income tax is that it is primarily a tax on the shareholders providing capital to the firm, rather than on the employees or customers of the corporation. A heavy, double tax on income from capital could have a serious effect on "capital formation." But, of course, whether it actually did or did not have this effect, it would almost certainly increase the political pressure for government intervention in the economy through direct spending programs, loan guarantees, or other forms of industrial policy.

Second, the partial exclusion of long-term capital gains is only in part intended as an incentive for capital investments. Another reason for the partial exclusion of these profits is the fact that some part of the nominal increase in value of long-held assets often reflects inflation rather than real profits. When inflation increases the price level by 5 percent, a share of stock bought at $100 and sold one year later at $105 has barely retained its real value. It certainly hasn't generated any real profits for the investor. Under the FAIR Tax, this stock transaction could generate a tax equal to 30 percent of the $5 gain, or $1.50, even though the investor is actually no better off. In fact, the investor would have been better advised to find something to *buy* for $100 before prices increased, rather than saving and investing, since the same item one year later will cost $105, and he will have only $103.50 after taxes. The absence of any relief for this taxation of purely nominal gains could create an incentive for taxpayers to consume *now*, rather than save and invest for subsequent consumption, since even purely inflationary gains will be fully taxed. This problem of indexing long-held investments for inflation is one of the most troubling problems in the income tax law. It is ignored by the FAIR Tax.

"FAST" AND LOOSE

The most prominent Republican alternative to the FAIR Tax of Democrats Bradley and Gephardt is the FAST tax sponsored by two conservative "supply side" Republicans, New York Congressman Jack Kemp and Wisconsin Senator Bob Kasten. FAST stands for the Fair And Simple Tax—goals that are obviously similar to the stated objectives of the FAIR Tax. The FAST Tax also broadens the tax base and lowers the tax rates, but it has some striking differences.

The basic structure of the FAST tax is different from current law in that there is only one tax bracket for all taxpayers. Everyone pays a flat 25 percent of their income in taxes. Well, almost. Families with less than $40,000 in income from wages and salaries get a special deduction equal to 20 percent of that income. The result is a tax rate that's really much lower for moderate-income families. The maximum benefit granted by this deduction is a tax reduction of $2,000. But the benefit is taken away as income rises above $40,000 until it disappears when income reaches about $100,000. So much for simplicity. The box below provides some examples of the plan's impact on moderate-income families.

What these examples illustrate is that neither of these income tax reforms make it very much simpler to compute individual tax liabilities.

FAST vs. FAIR

Both the FAIR tax and the FAST tax reduce taxes for very low income families, but the FAST tax goes further. Current law starts taxing a family of four with about $7,400 of income, and the FAIR tax starts at $11,200. But the FAST tax starts a little slower, exempting income up to $14,375. The FAST tax is also more generous to large, lower income families and single parents. That's because it provides about the same standard deduction as current law but much larger dependency exemptions for children. The FAST tax allows a $2,000 deduction for each dependent. The FAIR tax only allows the $1,000 permitted by current law.

A single parent with two children earning $15,000 would pay $825 in taxes under the FAST tax, a substantial reduction from the $1,359 required under current law. The FAIR tax would also reduce that family's tax burden, but only to $1,148. A lower income married couple with two children would find FAST much fairer than FAIR until their income reached around $22,000, when the two plans would both impose a tax of around $1,500, a $600 reduction compared to current law.

They both present the same choice as current law between standard deductions and itemizing, and have exemptions that vary with the individual family situation.

For the vast majority of taxpayers with incomes below $40,000 largely consisting of wage and salary income, the FAST tax pretty much preserves the status quo (like the FAIR tax). Deductions for mortgage interest, charitable deductions, state and local taxes, and major medical expenses are preserved, along with IRA and Keogh contributions. But these deductions are allowed without limitation, unlike the FAIR tax that allows the deductions only against the bottom 14 percent tax bracket. FAST also preserves indexing of the standard deductions, personal exemptions, and the earned income deduction to prevent inflation from raising taxes by diminishing the real value of these exempt amounts. (Since there's only one tax bracket, this problem can't be called bracket creep. At this point, we'll assume everyone understands the problem well enough without the need for a catchy new slogan.)

FAST and Investment Income

FAST breaks further away from both current law and the FAIR plan in its treatment of savings and investment income. The adoption of a single-bracket tax structure, with one, flat 25 percent tax rate, makes it more difficult to "soak the rich" (who generally save and invest larger portions of their income) by raising marginal tax rates. But just to be sure that saving and investment are not stifled by over-taxation, the FAST plan is more cautious in removing several of the tax preferences for investment. The investment tax credit for equipment and the credit for research and development expenses are repealed, but the accelerated cost recovery system for rapid depreciation of buildings and equipment is retained and extended to depletable resources like oil, gas, and mining. The corporate tax rate is reduced from 46 percent to 30 percent with a special 15 percent rate for the first $50,000 of corporate profits, presumably to assist smaller businesses.

FAST gradually eliminates the favored tax treatment of long-term capital gains realized by individuals (it is phased out over a 10-year period) but never requires taxes to be paid on purely inflationary gains. By adjusting or indexing the "cost" of a capital asset for inflation and allowing taxes to be deferred until the asset is sold, the plan preserves incentives for individuals to invest in corporate stock. In addition, the

FAST plan would allow unlimited amounts of real capital losses to be deducted from ordinary income, a valuable incentive for particularly risky investments.

One of the reasons for a flat 25 percent tax rate is the fact that neither Kemp nor Kasten favors increasing taxes above their present levels to reduce the deficit. With a flat, 25 percent tax rate and many investment tax preferences still retained (like accelerated cost recovery for real estate investments) the FAST tax could substantially reduce taxes for many higher income taxpayers. Nothing but the supply-sider's faith would guarantee that these tax savings would result in increased work, savings, and investment.

A WAR WAGED FOR THE SOUL OF THE INCOME TAX

Neither FAIR nor FAST dramatically simplifies the tax law for the majority of Americans—if what's meant by simplification is easing the annual process of filing a tax return. Both of these plans, as well as the more radical "really flat, true income" tax proposals, apparently mean something quite different when they talk about tax simplification.

These tax reform proposals attempt to simplify the *concept* of the income tax, to reduce the number of policies being served by the tax

---

"FAST III"

At the time this book went to press, Senator Bob Kasten and Congressman Jack Kemp had just introduced the *third* version of their FAST tax. Among the important changes is a reduction of the tax rate from 25 to 24 percent, elimination of full deductibility of capital losses against ordinary income, permanent preservation of the option to exclude 40 percent of long-term capital gains, and modification of the depreciation rules to increase the total amount of allowable deductions, but push them into future years, to avoid early revenue losses. Philosophically, these modifications are consistent with the approach taken in the earlier versions of the bill.

---

system, which will enable the average taxpayer to understand more easily how much he or she—and everyone else—is *really* expected to pay (and who's getting away with murder!).

Making the income tax rules more explicit is what FAIR and FAST really accomplish. But knowledge is power, and understanding can lead to change. That is why FAIR and FAST have staked out two realistic— but radically different positions on what the income tax should be.

FAIR preserves the existing moderately progressive distribution of income tax burdens for now, but it sets the stage for a dramatic increase in taxes on corporations and families with incomes above $40,000. It banishes virtually all savings and investment incentives from the tax code, creates some incentives for consumption, and allows even a modest amount of inflation to slowly remove the remaining tax subsidies for homeownership, charitable contributions, and major medical expenses. If these tax subsidies were *never* to be replaced with direct spending programs, then FAIR might well be the dream come true of a free-market conservative economist. But there is hardly any guarantee that it won't lead instead to a bureaucratic nightmare of massive governmental intervention in the economy.

FAST preserves a substantial amount of the progressivity of the current system and from one perspective increases it by lowering taxes on the working poor. But the rich are the beneficiaries of the plan's bold theorem that no one should ever pay more than a 25 percent marginal tax rate on income. More significant than any immediate tax reduction is the symbolic bulwark against "soaking the rich" created by the plan's flat 25 percent tax rate.

Whether the FAST tax plan's reduced tax rates and incentives for capital investment will help the entire economy—and whether Bradley-Gephardt's heavy taxation of capital will hurt the nation's competitiveness—are unanswered questions. Unfortunately, since the rich generally save and invest more of their income, the issue of tax incentives for savings, investment, and capital formation always seems to be mixed up with issues of "fairness" relating to "how much more" the rich should be forced to pay to support the government.

THE "WHAT THE HELL IS THAT?" TAX

Breaking this ideological stalemate is the goal of the third major type of income tax reform under serious discussion. It could well be called the "What the Hell Is That?" Tax since it is sometimes quite difficult to grasp what is really going on.

Imagine a retail sales tax on groceries that wasn't levied at a flat 5 or 6 percent on each package of soap or hotdogs, but grew larger the more you bought. A purchase of one bar of soap costing a dollar might produce a one percent, one penny tax, while a weekly shopping spree costing $100 would produce a 5 percent, $5 tax.

Now imagine that the tax was computed not on the basis of each individual trip to the supermarket, but on the basis of all the shopping you did at every supermarket, department store, and gas station during the year. (Obviously this sort of tax would be virtually impossible to enforce unless each of us was issued a single, national credit card for all purchases. But play along for a while—we're getting there.) This tax would be a tax on consumer spending that would encourage thrift, savings, and investment. But the tax would still be "progressive" in the sense that wealthier people (who consumed more) would pay "much more" than lower income families.

Finally, imagine that this sales tax wasn't computed just on the basis of a single year's shopping. But imagine that it was figured on a *lifetime* of shopping. You would never have a tax reason to buy now, rather than saving for the future, since your savings would never be taxed, but every single item of lifetime consumption would be. Got it?

Well, if the notion of paying taxes on what you consume or "take" from society (rather than what you save or "give") appeals to you, you probably would like this tax as a substitute for the income tax. It's been called a "Consumed Income Tax" or a "Cash Flow Expenditure Tax." (The names alone may convince you we've properly called it the "What the Hell Is That?" Tax.) It's obviously impossible to collect a sales tax that depends on the amount of purchases made at all supermarkets and stores in a week or a year, not to mention a lifetime. But almost the same effect can be obtained by making a relatively simple change to the current income tax.

The old joke about the income tax is that the new form has two lines: "How much did you make?" and "Send it in!" Under a consumed income tax the form would ask: "How much did you make?" "How much did you *save?*" "*Pay taxes only on what you didn't save!*" By allowing a full deduction from taxable income for all savings and invest-ment, the income tax can be converted into a tax only on the portion of income that is actually spent.

The incentive to save under this tax is dramatic. At the same time, wealthier people who are "big spenders" will pay "much more" as a percentage of their income and as a percentage of their annual spending than lower income families. The major advantage of this approach for advocates of a "soak the rich" tax policy is that it separates the "fairness" issue from the question of savings and investment incentives. A 50 percent tax on annual consumption in excess of $50,000 would be difficult to attack as a disincentive to savings and investment, since any income saved or invested would simply be tax-exempt.

At some point, of course, tax rates on consumption could become high enough to discourage work and investment (or to encourage an overthrow of the government by a well-financed group of conservative militants). But the "fairness" issue would have nothing to do with savings incentives: instead, it would be phrased as, "How much should the majority of middle-income taxpayers take from a wealthy minority before they can be rightfully accused of tyranny?"

Several versions of the consumed income tax have been introduced in Congress, and two scholars from the liberal Brookings Institution have also championed the cause. The idea is not really new. It was recommended as one of two serious tax reform options in a 1977 tax reform study performed by the Treasury Department under Secretary William E. Simon.

The consumed income tax is really an attempt to come to grips with the problem we identified back in Chapter 2, the strong but ambivalent feelings Americans have about savings, investment, and wealth. But not even all of the proponents of this approach to taxation can agree on a fundamental issue: should the tax system be used to prevent the accumulation and transfer by gift or inheritance of large family fortunes?

Taxing inheritances and taxing investment income have often been viewed as alternative ways of implementing the most traditional social goal of the federal income tax—preventing undue concentration of wealth and power among a small number of families or "dynasties." Two scholars from the Brookings Institution, Henry J. Aaron and Harvey Galper, concluded that no system should leave the wealthy completely free to pass on the untaxed fortune of a lifetime to the next generation. Their version of the consumed income tax would completely exempt each generation from taxation on its savings and investment income. But the plan would impose a double "consumption" tax on large inheritances and gifts.

Every gift (or bequest) larger than a specified exempt amount would be treated as "consumption" by the donor (or decedent) and taxed just as if he or she were purchasing a yacht or vacation home. The gift or bequest would then be treated as income to the recipient and taxed again. Of course, if the gift was immediately saved, the donee's tax would be deferred until the money was spent, or (you guessed it) given away. In effect, the income tax on savings and investment would not really be eliminated, but just deferred until the time a gift or bequest was made out of a previously untaxed family fortune.

Other versions of the consumed income tax, including the plans proposed by Democratic Congressman Cecil Heftel of Hawaii, lack this feature, and would impose only a single consumption tax on gifts and bequests (with no tax at all if the gift or bequest was saved and not spent).

Taxing inheritances is one of the most difficult issues for Congress, despite the fact that it generally entails very little tax revenue in the aggregate. (The current federal estate and gift taxes raise about $6 billion annually, less than one percent of total federal revenues.) It is unlikely that a double consumption tax on gifts and bequests would be imposed or retained in the law for very long. As a result, a consumed income tax is unlikely to be viewed as attractive to anyone who continues to be concerned about what has been called the "dynasty" problem of inherited wealth.

(If there truly were a consensus that heavy taxation of gifts and inheritances was the proper solution to our ambiguous feelings about savings, investment, and wealth, then it might make more sense to replace income taxation with a simple sales tax and a much more rigorous tax on gifts and bequests. That would avoid the problems relating to savings incentives and measurement of business income involved in the income tax, without the new problems of a consumed income tax.)

Although it may sound simple to allow a tax deduction for savings, the consumed income tax would have some truly bizarre features. For one thing, borrowed money would be treated as income. That means if a taxpayer was unemployed or in school, had no income, and borrowed and spent $20,000, that person would be taxed just as if he or she had earned and spent a $20,000 salary. When the loan was repaid, both interest and principal would be deductible—since the repayment of a debt is not considered "consumption."

If individuals earning $75,000 invested $50,000 of their earnings in corporate stock, they would be taxed only on the $25,000 that was left for "consumption," the same as wage earners who spent all of their $25,000 salary. This is because a $50,000 investment in the stock market would be a tax deductible item. But if the stock was later sold for $55,000, the entire $55,000 would be treated as income—and taxed unless it was reinvested.

This approach entirely eliminates the problem of taxing artificial gains attributable to inflation. As a result, if stock prices rise by 10 percent simply because the prices of food, clothing, and automobiles have also risen by 10 percent, then the taxpayer is no worse off for having invested instead of having consumed.

A consumed income tax offers great advantages for simplifying the taxation of business income. Depreciation would simply not exist, since the entire amount of any investment could be deducted. But borrowed money would be treated as income, just as repayments of debt would be fully deductible. Under some versions of the consumed income tax, including that proposed by the Treasury Department in 1977, the corporate income tax could be eliminated, except as a way of ensuring that corporations did not disguise fringe benefits (consumption) as business expenses that avoided the individual tax on "consumption." A corporate tax might also be needed to prevent foreigners investing in U.S. corporations from completely avoiding U.S. taxation.

The consumed income tax equalizes the treatment of different kinds of investment by making it all tax-exempt—until it is spent. Industries that are subsidized by an unusually low (or negative) tax rate on investment would lose their competitive advantage. And tax-exempt municipal bonds would lose their appeal as tax shelters, since *any* bond would be tax-exempt as long as the interest income was not spent—and no bond would be tax-exempt if the interest income *was* spent. The problem of adjusting depreciation allowances, capital gains and losses, and interest payments for inflation would disappear, because of the focus of the tax on cash flow rather than income.

A consumed income tax can exempt certain kinds of personal consumption, just as the income tax allows deductions for certain kinds of expenses. For example, Congressman Heftel's bill would allow deductions for home mortgage interest, state and local income taxes, charitable contributions, and certain medical expenses. *Borrowing* for a home mortgage would also be exempt from the general rule that *borrowed money* is considered taxable income. In this way, the exalted position of owner-occupied housing would be preserved.

The biggest drawbacks to a consumed income tax are probably the transitional issues. Heavily tax-favored industries might experience dramatic declines in the value of existing properties. Individuals with accumulated savings that were previously subject to a full income tax could experience unfair double taxation if their savings (from the era of the old income tax) were taxed again when spent in the brave new world of the consumed income tax. And just to enforce the rule, a national inventory of personal assets might be required to prevent the establishment of a permanent underground economy of hidden wealth.

On the other hand, if all existing savings were exempted from tax, problems would also arise. Exemptions for existing wealth could lead to a situation where a large number of wealthy, big spenders paid little or no taxes. Finally, problems of complexity and poor taxpayer compliance could actually be aggravated by the transition to a new system with rules that might be perceived as truly bizarre—such as the taxation

---

SOMETHING INVESTED—NOTHING GAINED

An example may be helpful to illustrate the somewhat complex point that a consumed income tax eliminates the taxation of purely inflationary gains. A taxpayer earning $50,000 and saving $10,000 would be taxed on only $40,000. At a 20 percent tax rate, his tax savings from investing $10,000 would be $2,000. One year later, with 10 percent inflation, the price of a $10,000 automobile he had considered buying might have risen to $11,000. If his savings had barely kept up with inflation in a 10 percent savings account, the $10,000 saved would now be worth $11,000. Drawing down $11,000 of savings to buy the car would produce a 20 percent tax on $11,000 or $2,200. The added $200 of taxes is exactly what he was able to earn by investing his $2,000 of tax savings from the first year in the 10 percent account. Had he bought the car the first year, he would have paid $2,000 more in taxes a year earlier and not been able to earn the $200 of interest. With an income tax that does not allow a deduction for savings, he would be worse off by saving than if he had bought the car in the first year.

of borrowed money as "income" and the virtual exemption from tax of the wealthy but frugal miser.

Some aspects of the consumed income tax are already part of the tax law—such as the tax deduction for contributions to pension funds and Individual Retirement Accounts with full taxation only when the amounts are withdrawn. Gradual movement toward a consumed income tax could be made by adopting a comprehensive income tax (like that proposed by Secretary Regan or the Bradley-Gephardt plan) with greatly expanded provisions for tax deductible investment accounts (like IRA accounts). For example, the Bradley-Gephardt surtaxes could be increased, while permitting individuals to deduct large amounts contributed to tax-deferred savings accounts. The result, of course, would be a tax system very much like our present one (high tax rates, but exemptions for much investment income), except for the fact that the decision of what particular investment to place in the tax-exempt account would be left to the individual, rather than having the politicians in Washington decide which investments should enjoy tax subsidies.

This approach is similar to a tax reform plan proposed by Senator William Roth (R., DE) and Congressman W. Henson Moore (R., LA). The hallmark of the Roth-Moore plan is the creation of a tax-free investment account, called a Super Savings Account. Taxpayers would be permitted to deposit $10,000 each year ($20,000 for a married couple) for savings or investment. Amounts contributed to the account would be deductible and free from taxation. Only amounts withdrawn would be taxed. But to pay for this generous treatment of savings and investment, the income tax rates under the Roth-Moore plan cannot be reduced as fast as under the Bradley-Gephardt, Kemp-Kasten, or Treasury Department plan.

6

Doctor Regan's Prescription

The Treasury report was so long that some lobbyists called it "The Treasury Department Miniseries." In fact, when the typesetting on this manuscript began, the last installment of Secretary Regan's three-volume report to the President had not yet been released. To add to the suspense—as we went to press—nobody knew whether the President would endorse or reject the Treasury proposal.

Both Secretary Regan and the President praised the document, while indicating that changes might be made. But even if modified, the original report will still be viewed as reflecting the Treasury Department's best professional judgment on the issues of tax reform, whatever positions Secretary Regan or President Reagan may later take.

The Treasury's announced aim was to fulfill President Ronald Reagan's request in his 1984 State of the Union message for tax proposals that would promote fairness, simplicity, and economic growth. The Treasury staff considered four major tax reform alternatives: a pure flat tax (the Really Flat, True Income Tax described on page 26), a modified flat tax (similar to the Bradley-Gephardt and Kemp-Kasten described on pages 65 to 76), a consumed income tax (the "What the Hell Is That" Tax, described on page 76), and a sales tax (which might be structured either like the Invisible Flat Tax described on page 41, or the "One Day at a Time" Flat Tax described on page 36).

The Treasury's recommendation of a modified flat tax came as no real surprise. Prominent supply-side Republicans and liberal Democrats had both trailblazed their own versions with largely positive reactions. So the political risk of offering yet another variation on the theme was minimal. Curiously, although a sales tax was among the rejected options, the Treasury devoted a full volume of its three-part saga to discussing a VAT. To some observers, it seemed a little like saying, "Don't think about elephants."

THE END OF INDUSTRIAL POLICY?

Critics, at first, said the plan would never be endorsed by the President, since it proposed to eliminate the business tax breaks cherished by many of his most devoted supporters. But on deeper reflection, the plan was profoundly in tune with a fundamental and recurring theme of the Reagan presidency—getting the government out of the private economy and allowing the marketplace to function freely (for better or worse).

Indeed, the Treasury plan was almost foreshadowed by the President's Address to the Congress on February 18, 1981, when he stated:

> The taxing power of government must be used to provide revenues for legitimate government purposes. It must not be used to regulate the economy or bring about social change. We've tried that, and surely we must be able to see it doesn't work.

Back in Chapter 3, we looked at several public opinion polls about the tax system. One important question is always missing from surveys of this sort: "Is the purpose of the tax code to raise needed revenue for government programs, or is the purpose to target and direct the investment dollars of wealthy individuals and corporations?"

If Lou Harris went around asking questions like that, most people would think he was pulling their leg. After all, it is called the Internal *Revenue* Code, not the Internal *Investment* Code. But this question is at the heart of the controversy surrounding the Regan proposal. To understand quickly where the Treasury Department is coming from, you may want to glance at the tables on pages 119 to 121, which show the vastly different effective tax rates of large corporations in different industries.

Is it the economic policy of the United States to direct investment dollars *away* from companies like Procter and Gamble, United Parcel Service, Eastman Kodak, and R.J. Reynolds—and to funnel *more* capital into companies like General Electric, Ford Motor Company, AT&T, and Union Carbide? If this is our policy, when was the policy decision made, and how did your Congressperson vote? If not, why is the effective tax rate on the soap and cosmetic industry so much higher than the average, and that on the chemical industry so low?

The answers to these questions can be found scattered through the past 70 years of congressional history. Sometimes intentionally, sometimes inadvertently, Congress granted special deductions, exemptions, and credits that served to reduce or eliminate the *taxable* income of certain businesses, even when those businesses were extremely profitable. No one in Congress or in any government department really knows how all these different provisions interact to influence private investment decisions. But the bottom line is an industrial policy for corporate America to the tune of $94 billion in 1985 alone.

How does it work? Here's an example. You start with a corporate tax rate of 46 percent. Then you introduce fast depreciation write-offs and investment tax credits to spur investment in new equipment. *Voila!* If a company is investing in new machinery, its *real* tax rate drops below 46 percent.

If the competition is trying to improve its own productivity with better management and employee training programs (instead of new machinery)—well, they're stuck. So you decide that the situation just isn't fair, or that it's not good for labor. The answer? You give the *second* company a tax credit for hiring disadvantaged workers, and you grant a tax exemption for the expenses of training existing employees for new, more responsible positions. Okay. Their real tax rate drops, too, although not by as much.

Then you hear from the high-tech boys, and decide that what the country *really* needs isn't a good 50 cent cigar, but a new 2 cent microchip, and that a special tax credit for "research and development" will hasten its arrival. Get the picture?

That's the way the system "works." What's wrong with it? Maybe nothing. Maybe a lot.

If you're an economic conservative who believes that the marketplace (not government) should decide where the most productive investments are, then it doesn't make much sense to have a $94 billion corporate industrial policy imbedded in the tax code.

If you're an economic interventionist who believes in establishing a rational, centrally controlled, politically responsive industrial policy, then you've got to be offended by the sheer chaos of the Internal Revenue Code.

And if you're not exactly sure what you want, except that you would like to be able to understand whether there is an industrial policy being proposed or pursued, then you just might prefer having that done clearly and explicitly (perhaps through a direct subsidy, or a loan guarantee program similar to the "bail outs" used to aid Chrysler or the City of New York).

Any one of these different political theories can explain the Treasury Department's plan for business taxation. Simply stated, the idea is to make *taxable* income as close to real *economic* income as possible by repealing almost all of the tax expenditures and special incentives in the tax code. Once you eliminate preferential treatment for certain privileged forms of income, the tax rates can be brought down for everyone.

The Treasury Department's "hit list" of tax expenditures is similar to that contained in the Bradley-Gephardt and Kemp-Kasten tax plans, only much more comprehensive. After broadening the corporate tax base, the tax rates are then dropped from the current 46 percent to 33 percent. If you have any doubts how much is being given away in tax expenditures, just keep in mind that this substantial rate reduction actually results in a tax *increase* for the entire corporate sector of about 25 percent!

Under the Treasury plan, corporations are also partially relieved of the double taxation of corporate dividends. Complete elimination of this two-tier tax (once on the corporation when its profits are earned, again when dividends are distributed to the shareholders) is something the Treasury tax planners hoped to achieve, but just couldn't afford right away. Their stated reasons for eliminating the double taxation dramatically illustrates the philosophy of free-market economics that pervades the report.

When a tax system discourages dividends, corporations are given an incentive to finance their growth and expansion out of the profits they *retain*, rather than distributing those profits currently to their shareholders. Shareholders are generally more than happy to comply, since they anticipate the prospect of selling their shares in a growing company and paying only a capital gains tax on the profits. (And if the shares are passed on at death, the capital gains tax is forgiven!)

But this system deprives the shareholders of any direct control over the choice of *whether* to reinvest, and *how* to reinvest their share of the company's annual earnings. Instead, corporate management makes the choice. The discipline of proxy fights, tender offers, and takeover battles is present, of course. But these tools are cumbersome and haphazard when compared with the prospect of corporations actually distributing their annual earnings, and having to convince existing shareholders to lend or reinvest additional money with the company.

By allowing a partial deduction for dividends (and perhaps ultimately a full deduction), the tax system would encourage dividend distributions. As a result, the annual earnings of corporate America would be regularly run through the gauntlet of the capital markets, with all of the accompanying risks and opportunities. The risks may be that a declining management team may have less access to investment capital. The opportunities may include easier access to capital for a start-up company with a better mousetrap.

As the report explains,

> Corporations will . . . be more subject to the discipline of the marketplace and less likely to make relatively unproductive investments simply because they have available funds. Similarly, the pool of funds available to new firms with relatively high productivity investment opportunities will be larger. As a result, the productivity of investment should be improved substantially.

THE END OF TAX SHELTERS?

Removing industrial policy from the tax code means that each investment will have to sink or swim on its own, without government assistance in the form of tax deductions for "artificial losses"—such as depreciation deductions for buildings that aren't really declining in value, or the immediate deduction of oil-drilling costs that should properly be matched against the income later produced by a successful well. Many start-up companies will continue to generate real losses in their early years. But artificial losses would no longer be generated by profitable investments, solely as a way of attracting investment dollars from doctors, lawyers, and movie stars desperately in need of tax losses to shelter their incomes from the ravages of the 50 percent marginal tax rate.

Beyond repealing the deductions and credits that produce these artificial losses, the Treasury plan would virtually eliminate the most common investment vehicle for distributing the losses to investors. Partnerships with more than 35 limited partners (investors who share profits and tax losses, but not real economic losses beyond their initial investment) would be taxed as corporations and prohibited from passing on any tax benefits to passive investors. In addition, both the investment interest rules and the "at risk" rules that limit deductions by tax shelter investors would be tightened.

Much of the existing real estate market is built on subsidies provided by artificial losses that are passed through large partnerships to multitudes of passive investors. One of the most provocative political questions raised by these changes is whether residential rents will rise. And if they do, will Congress or local governments respond with increased housing subsidies or some form of rent control?

Residential rental property is not the only heavily tax-subsidized industry in the country, and rental developers could benefit from the increased capital flows freed up from other tax-subsidized activities, such as equipment leasing. But the Treasury report offers no economic analysis or prediction on this point.

NOT THE END OF INFLATION?

In one respect, the Treasury's proposed curtailment of existing tax benefits for capital investment may be much less than meets the eye. The proposal does tax capital gains as ordinary income, repeals the investment tax credit, stretches out depreciation deductions, and repeals percentage depletion of certain oil and mineral resources. But in each of these areas, the Treasury plan "giveth" as well as "taketh away." (That is, at least if you are among those who believe that our country's inflation problems have not necessarily been licked for all time.)

Historically, the lower tax rate for capital gains had nothing to do with inflation. The low rate was intended as a crude form of "income averaging" to prevent the accumulated profits of several years from being taxed at artificially high marginal rates, when the gains were recognized all in one year. But one of the more recent justifications for the capital gains preference is the avoidance of taxation on purely inflationary gains, when stock or property has not gained in value but has merely kept up with general price inflation.

Similarly, the generous depreciation provisions of the Accelerated Cost Recovery System enacted in 1981, together with the investment tax credit, were justified not only as a spur to capital investment, but as a crude form of "insurance" that inflation would not erode the value of depreciation deductions and result in excessive taxation of the income generated by capital investments.

To remedy these and other problems caused by the past failures of the tax code to deal with inflation, the Treasury plan would establish a complex system of *indexing* capital assets, depreciation deductions, inventories, and even interest income and expenses, against the ravages of inflation.

Obviously, the implication is that inflation has not been permanently licked. And the argument is advanced quite persuasively that at *high* rates of inflation the Treasury proposal may be more generous than current law for investors in capital assets. But in most cases, the relative tax incentive to invest in plant and equipment is reduced.

On the other hand, under the Treasury plan investors are effectively insured against the over-taxation of capital investments and guaranteed a level paying field in the tax law, without regard to the policies of the Federal Reserve Board or the Organization of Petroleum Exporting Countries.

If you believe that business responds better to certainty and predictability than it does to tax incentives that may be extravagant one day and niggardly the next, you may agree that the Treasury proposal will, over time, produce a better climate for increased saving and investment. Of course, the Treasury could have recommended a plan that was not only inflation proof, but also created substantial incentives for capital investment. That's exactly what the consumption taxes described in Chapter 3 and the consumed income tax (described on page 77) would do.

WHAT ABOUT INDIVIDUALS?

For individuals, the Treasury plan is similar to the Bradley-Gephardt and Kemp-Kasten tax reform proposals. Tax rates are dramatically reduced in a system that would have only three tax brackets: 15 percent, 25 percent, and 35 percent. By increasing the individual personal exemption from $1,000 to $2,000 and increasing the current "zero bracket amount" (what used to be called the "standard deduction"), nearly all families with incomes below the official poverty level will be exempted from income taxation. In addition, of the approximately 34 million taxpayers who now itemize deductions, about 10 million will find it just as advantageous to file the short form. While the mortgage interest deduction would be retained, consumer interest deductions would be limited, and no deductions would be permitted for state and local taxes of any kind.

The entire proposal is summarized and compared with other tax reform plans in Appendix E. A few key points are worth stressing.

The plan claims to preserve the existing progressivity of the individual tax system and would actually reduce individual taxes overall (at the expense of corporations) by about 8.5 percent. But the most aggressive tax shelter investors (in any given income class) would probably pay more taxes, while those (in any given income class) who live out their lives oblivious to the inurements of the tax code will probably pay much less.

The plan pays homage to the goal of tax simplifications for individuals in at least two time-tested ways. First, it simply eliminates many tax deductions that involve difficult record-keeping problems for individuals. For example, it denies deductions for sales taxes (along with other state and local taxes) and allows charitable contribution deductions only when they exceed 2 percent of the taxpayer's income (about $500 for the median family of four).

This is an example of the so-called "nuisance-envy" theory of tax simplification: the theory that most taxpayers would just as soon give up a bothersome deduction—as long as they are sure no one else is claiming it. The Treasury Department estimates that this change will eliminate the "nuisance" of itemizing charitable gifts for about half of the taxpayers who currently do so (presumably without any significant increase in "taxpayer envy").

The second time-tested method of promoting tax simplification is to ask for a study. The Treasury Department study explains that the IRS will itself be studying a "return-free" tax system where, for simple returns, the IRS would replace the local tax-return preparer and send a completed form to individuals for their approval and signature. (In fairness, no comment is offered here, pending release of the forthcoming IRS study.)

AFTERMATH: ECONOMIC RENAISSANCE OR "ECONOMIC WINTER"?

It's hard for an American businessperson to disagree with the notion of a free economic marketplace, with minimal government intervention. That notion is the very cornerstone of the American business creed. It is hard to disagree—but not impossible.

Conversely, it is almost impossible for the Washington representative of a powerful trade, labor, charity, or industry group to *agree* with the notion of a free economic marketplace, with minimal government intervention. For that notion may be perceived as a ticket to the unemployment line.

Few industries will be as vocal as the National Association of Realtors in demanding that they be compensated—not for the denial of a tax deduction or credit—but for the mere lowering of marginal tax rates across the board. One week before the Treasury plan was released, the president of the "world's largest trade association" wrote the President of the United States, explaining that a reduction in personal income tax rates from 34 percent to 29 percent would reduce the incentive for homeownership created by the mortgage interest deduction by about $420 for a typical family. The letter continued:

> Therefore, an equal or greater incentive should be provided by other provisions equal to or greater than the $420 incentive lost by across-the-board tax cuts. The $420 loss of incentive for homeowners is equivalent to increasing interest rates for homeowners by .7 percentage points, which would cause 350,000 fewer families to satisfy their home needs each year.

Some heavily tax-subsidized industries may view the Treasury proposal as the economic equivalent of a nuclear first strike. Most businessmen, however, probably will conclude that, given time, they can survive the Treasury's massive retaliation against the tax preferences of the Internal Revenue Code. But a critical question posed by the Treasury proposal pertains to the short- and medium-term effects of a sudden return to economic reality.

Even if the plan is "survivable," will it lead to an "economic winter" where clouds of uncertainty and investor confusion prevent the rapid re-establishment of a vibrant economic system based on free enterprise? Are individual investors so hooked on tax breaks as an incentive for risk taking that they will be unwilling to invest in anything other than Treasury bills and other safe, interest-bearing securities? In short, has the tax system so poisoned the traditional calculus of investor risks and rewards that tax reform will leave us without the entrepreneurial drive to compete against the non-Yankee ingenuity of our foreign trading partners?

If these are perceived as realistic problems, then a more gradual approach may be warranted. But if we conclude that American businessmen and investors need a *permanent* government incentive to take private risks, then the Treasury Department proposal should be sent back to the drawing board.

7

A Chapter For
the Wealthy

This chapter is intended only for the wealthy. Well, all right. You can also read it if you *expect* to be wealthy someday. Or even if you really, truly want to be wealthy. But that's it. No one else should waste their time.

The most effective strategy for surviving tax reform is probably pretty much the same for all of you. There really isn't any air-tight evidence on whether increased tax rates on savings and investment will hurt the economy and reduce our international competitiveness. But emphasizing the importance of tax incentives for savings and capital formation is probably the best way to keep effective tax rates lower for higher income people. It also may be the best way to make it possible for people without wealth to get it.

The wealthy and the potentially wealthy are perfect allies in the battle over tax reform. Sensitizing lower and middle-income people to the "risk of wealth"—the possibility that they could make a killing in the stock market, start their own successful business, write a best-selling novel, or even just save and build up equity in a personal residence—is the best antidote to the leveling, egalitarian impulse lurking in our democracy.

Whatever you do, don't fall into the trap of supporting a tax reform plan that lowers the statutory tax rates much below 50 percent without any special tax incentives for savings, investment, or capital gains. The low rates won't last. And once Congress goes through the wrenching process of removing investment tax preferences from the tax code, it may take a generation before they can be put back. Even a tax plan like the Kemp-Kasten FAST tax, with a flat 25 percent tax rate, is too risky.

The FAST tax is viewed as giving some tax relief *now* to the highest income taxpayers and as being less vulnerable to a later rate increase because of its single, flat rate. But don't kid yourself. A steep, high-income surtax is just as possible with the FAST plan as with the Bradley-Gephardt FAIR tax. In fact, the absence of any provision in the Bradley-Gephardt plan for indexing the tax brackets for inflation is the one positive feature from your perspective. The impact of bracket creep will be much more serious on lower income taxpayers. And the automatic tax increases provided by inflation-caused bracket creep may provide enough of a stream of increasing revenues to preclude, or at least limit, any major increase in the surtax on higher income taxpayers.

A 50 percent tax rate is a good, round number that seems to strike most people as a reasonable upper limit on the amount the government should take. And since 1978, when the amount of exempt capital gains was raised from 50 percent of the profit on a sale to 60 percent, popular support for savings incentives, tax-free savings accounts, and lower tax rates for investment earnings has only increased. A 50 percent tax rate, with an across-the-board exclusion of, say, half of all investment income, is much more stable and more politically defensible than a 30 percent maximum tax rate with all income taxed alike.

An explicit, across-the-board preference for *all* income from savings and investment is probably better than the patchwork of investment subsidies now in the tax law. Simplifying the rules and making the major savings incentive something everyone with a bank account can understand and use should please both the masses and the academic tax purists.

Some tax increases may be necessary in the next few years, and you should be more than willing to pay your fair share as long as the current distribution of tax burdens is maintained. According to the estimates of the Congressional Joint Committee on Taxation, the average income-tax rate of the very wealthiest taxpayers with incomes over $200,000 per year is now about 25 percent. If it comes down to a debate over effective tax rates, be sure to point out that this is about double the average tax rate for all taxpayers (around 12.3 percent) and more than twice the 10.6 percent rate for the biggest group of taxpayers, those earning between $20,000 and $30,000. (The Treasury Department's statistics on tax rates as a percentage of real economic income are somewhat lower, but their view of the progressivity of the system is about the same, with the wealthiest paying 21 percent and the average taxpayer paying only about 9 percent.)

All things considered, it's probably best to use absolute dollar figures in any debate over the "fairness" of the tax system. Ask your opponents if it's an "unfair" tax system that makes taxpayers earning $150,000 pay an average income tax bill of $34,000, when the average American earning $25,000 pays only $2,650. If that doesn't work, try to deflect any tax increases to the corporate tax.

Now, no one knows with certainty, but an income tax on business corporations is mostly thought to be a tax on shareholders, and only partially a tax that is reflected in increased prices for consumer goods or reduced wages for corporate employees. But to some extent the tax may be reflected in reduced wage levels and increased prices of consumer products. Liberal defenders of the supposed interests of labor and lower income consumers often refuse to even admit this possibility, so it's probably best to cut your losses, accept a high effective tax rate on corporations, and hope that more of the tax is reflected in consumer prices and wage levels.

Of course, don't give up without a good debate. The major reason for the recent decline in corporate taxes paid as a percentage of actual profits is the generous capital recovery allowances permitted by the investment tax credit and the accelerated cost recovery system adopted in 1981. The key point to make here is that these allowances are generous only if inflation continues to remain low. If any changes in cost recovery are proposed to increase the corporate tax, insist on adjusting the capital recovery allowances for inflation to ensure that reasonable depreciation deductions agreed upon today don't lose their value if inflation goes up.

Interest expenses and income would also need to be adjusted for inflation to make the system work perfectly. Indexing interest expenses, interest income, and depreciation allowances could be very difficult to implement—both technically and politically, even though the Treasury Department has proposed such a system in its report.

If a corporate tax increase is inevitable, or if you decide to promote one in order to deflect attention from the level of individual taxes paid by high-income taxpayers, be sure to raise the issue of double taxation on corporate income. The profits of corporations are taxed once at the corporate level (except on certain new capital investments where the depreciation allowances are generous enough to zero-out any real tax burden) and once again when the profits are distributed as dividends.

Numerous proposals have been advanced to eliminate this double taxation by "integrating" the corporate and individual taxes. The basic idea is that corporations would pay a tax on income but claim a deduction for dividends so that the dividends are not taxed twice. Another approach is to give shareholders a tax credit for their share of the taxes paid by the corporation. The Treasury Department has proposed partial integration that would be accomplished with a deduction for half of all dividends paid.

From your perspective, the deductible dividend approach is probably better. Hopefully, the public would soon come to understand that corporations were only expected to pay taxes on the earnings they didn't distribute to investors. The shareholder credit approach is preferred by a number of tax experts. But you wouldn't want to find yourself having to defend the legitimacy of claiming all those tax credits on your own individual tax return. (Face it, Congress is fickle. What they say is "legitimate" one day may be considered an "abuse" the next.)

An integrated, inflation-proof corporate tax with tax rates no higher than 50 percent, together with a 50 percent maximum individual tax rate and an across-the-board individual exemption of some portion of all investment income (like the current exclusion of 60 percent of long-term capital gains), is the best income tax system you could hope for.

Your greatest opponents may be the state and local issuers of tax-exempt municipal bonds who want to preserve their exemption while fully taxing all other investment income. The municipal bond lobby could be appeased by the high tax rates you want, if the percentage of other investment income that is exempt is kept low.

Your greatest ally may be the universities, art museums, and other "upper class" charities who depend on high tax rates and the charitable deduction to preserve a high level of contributions.

8

Soaking the Rich

SOAKING INDIVIDUALS

If the tax reform strategy you want to pursue is "soaking the rich"—drastically increasing taxes on very high income Americans to reduce the burden on low and moderate-income taxpayers—there's good news and bad news. The good news is that very wealthy families could be made to pay higher taxes, probably without any serious damage to the economy. The bad news is that there's not enough money to be gotten from that strategy to significantly reduce or relieve the income tax burden on the majority of lower and middle-income taxpayers.

That doesn't necessarily mean you shouldn't pursue your strategy for other reasons. Belief in the goal of a more egalitarian society where the fortunate are not very much better off materially than the less fortunate may provide all the motivation you need. Unfortunately, soaking the rich through higher income taxes may be a difficult strategy to implement politically, if it doesn't do anything very *positive* for lower and middle-income taxpayers.

The Census Bureau and the Internal Revenue Service recently released comprehensive data on the distribution of tax liabilities among families of differing incomes for 1981. The tax cuts of the 1981 Tax Act and the cutbacks in tax shelters enacted in 1982 and 1984 are not reflected in these statistics, but they still provide a pretty accurate overall view of the situation, even now.

In 1981, there were around 83 million American households. The four-person family had a median income of $26,324, which means that half of the families earned less than that and half earned more. Keeping that figure in mind, let's take a look at public attitudes about the tax burden of the rich, the poor, and the middle class.

A 1979 poll conducted by H&R Block, the tax return preparers, found that more than 70 percent of the public feels that "middle income" families pay too much taxes and "high income" families pay too little income taxes. Views about "low income" families were somewhat less dramatic. About 45 percent of the respondents thought that "low income" families paid too much, but 38 percent felt they were paying "about the right amount" of income taxes.

Understandably, respondents with incomes below $7,000 were much more convinced that low-income families paid too much. Sixty-one percent of that group said they paid "too much" and only 26 percent thought what they were paying was "about right." Taxpayers earning less than $10,000 will contribute less than 2 percent of the $296 billion of individual income taxes to be collected in 1984. Providing this group with complete income tax relief would not be that costly. But it would increase their after-tax incomes by less than 5 percent. If income redistribution is your goal, you may want to consider seriously whether to concentrate on income tax reductions or on increases in noncash benefits like food stamps and housing assistance.

Obviously, the real action is with the "middle income" taxpayers who are convinced they pay "too much" because the wealthy pay "too little." But the same H&R Block study asked the respondents to draw the line between what they considered to be a "low," "middle," and "high" income for a family of four. The average response in 1979 was that low-income families were those earning less than $20,679, and high-income families were those earning more than $42,939. Adjusting these 1979 responses to current median income data, it's reasonable to conclude that the biggest block of voters today believe that the "rich" who are paying too little are those earning more than $60,000, and the "middle income" who deserve tax relief are those earning between $20,000 and $50,000.

The biggest problem in any effort to "soak the rich" is convincing the majority of middle income voters that you have properly focused your aim on the "truly rich," a concept that may be as elusive as the "truly needy." Just to be on the safe side politically, let's use a round number of $100,000 in annual income in defining the "rich" and $200,000 in income for the "filthy rich."

According to estimates prepared by the Congressional Joint Committee on taxation, the "rich" now pay around 22 percent of their "expanded income" in income taxes and the "filthy rich" around 25 percent. "Expanded income" is a rough surrogate for economic income that takes adjusted gross income shown on tax returns and adds back various tax preferences like the exempt portion of long-term capital gains.

(Compared with true economic income, these average tax-rate figures are a little high. According to the Treasury Department report to the President, the "rich" now pay around 13 percent and the "filthy rich" pay around 21 percent of their economic income in taxes. But don't jump to conclusions. Using "economic income," the Treasury concludes that middle-income families earning between $30,000 and $50,000 pay less than 8 percent.)

Treasury Department projections indicate that the rich and filthy rich will contribute about 27 percent of the income taxes to be collected in 1986 (even though they will be earning less than 15 percent of the total adjusted gross income on which the tax is based). That will mean a total contribution of slightly more than $100 billion into a total pot of $375 billion collected from individual income taxes. If taxes on the rich and filthy rich were doubled, their tax rates would rise to around 40 percent. That extreme measure would raise $100 billion. But with a deficit of $200 billion, and talk of the need for a tax increase to cover at least half of that, $100 billion is simply not enough money to provide any meaningful tax reduction to low- and middle-income families.

Of course, short of a major war or environmental disaster, a 100 percent tax increase, even for the rich and filthy rich, is slightly unrealistic. A 20 percent increase for the rich and a 30 percent increase for the filthy rich (still quite an optimistic goal) might raise only $25 billion. In short, whether or not it's a good or bad idea from the standpoint of fairness, equity, or economic policy, soaking the rich is not likely to resolve the problems of complexity and perceived burdensomeness and unfairness of the income tax.

That doesn't mean the tax system cannot be made simpler or more fair. But it is already doubtful that most Americans realize that the rich pay as much taxes as they do. In 1981, the filthy rich earned an average "expanded income" of about $450,000 and paid an average federal income tax of $135,000. Even after the tax cuts of 1981, the average tax paid by a filthy rich person earning $450,000 will be more than $94,000 in 1985. The gap between perceptions and reality raises questions about whether any income tax levied on lower- and middle-income families will ever be perceived as fair, regardless of what the "experts" and the cold statistics say.

SOAKING THE RICH CORPORATIONS

If you want to soak the rich corporations, the first question you must answer is whether what you care about is having the corporations actually writing the checks to Uncle Sam, or what you really want is a tax on the income earned by individuals who own corporate stock—who are generally wealthier than average tax payers. If it's just a matter of having the corporations writing the checks—so that massive amounts of revenue can be raised in a relatively painless way (perhaps to fund large spending programs for the lower and middle classes)—then a value-added tax is really your best bet. One corporate lobbyist has even been promoting a value-added tax that exempts retail operations. Called a "tax on business transactions," it is even "more invisible" than a regular VAT.

If what you want instead is heavier taxation of the individual shareholders who own the corporations, you will have to confront all the old arguments about the double taxation of corporate profits, along with the arguments about the effects that heavy taxation of investment income will have on capital formation and a healthy economy.

If this is what you really want, then the best approach may be a two-step strategy. First, get the tax system working "right" to equalize the treatment of wage and investment income. That probably means working hard for enactment of something very much like the Treasury Department proposal. The next step is to increase the top individual and corporate tax rates. If you wait until the right time to pounce (a national emergency or a fiscal crisis), you may be very successful in increasing the progressivity of the tax system. But don't try to raise the rates until you're sure all the "holes" are plugged. Otherwise, it will be like bailing out a dinghy with a spaghetti strainer.

9

The Loophole Mongers

"I'M MAD AS HELL AND I'M NOT GOING TO TAKE IT ANYMORE"

If what you want is neither to soak the rich, nor to become one of them, but just to get rid of the headaches of individual income taxation for the low- and middle-income taxpayers, good luck.

It's not that an armistice couldn't be worked out between the rich, poor, and middle classes. It's just that the "loophole mongers"—everyone from the real estate agents (who belong to "the world's largest trade association") to the physicians who want to keep generous health insurance premiums exempt from taxation—have a very strong interest in preserving the status quo. Their goal is to preserve the income tax as a tax on middle-income Americans, with exemptions for everything from middle-income mortgage interest deductions, to middle-income health insurance premiums and middle-income retirement plans.

It's hard to say that high levels of homeownership, medical insurance coverage, and private pension coverage are terrible things. Pensions and medical insurance could be required without government subsidies, and homeownership subsidies could be provided through existing mechanisms for government-insured mortgages. But, of course, that's not going to happen over night.

To get any long-lasting relief from the hassles of the current system, we would need to replace the income tax on low- and middle-income families with a VAT or national sales tax. It wouldn't be easy to enact even a one percent tax on consumer spending, but that may be all that's needed to start the ball rolling. If a sales tax were linked to a special surtax on the incomes of high-income taxpayers, then both rates could gradually be ratcheted up together, as the regular income tax was gradually eliminated.

In 10 or 20 years, what might be left would be a broad-based 20 percent national sales tax or value added tax (possibly raising around $360 billion in 1984 dollars), a flat 20 percent income tax on all wage and investment income in excess of $50,000 (possibly raising around $50 billion), and a flat 20 percent tax on corporate economic profits (possibly raising around $44 billion). If this 20-20-20 consensus could be established, all three tax rates would be linked, and no tax would be raised or lowered without the others. Something like this is really the only possible strategy for combining simplification for the vast majority of individuals with a distribution of tax burdens viewed as reasonably fair by liberals and conservatives.

These estimates are very rough, back-of-the-envelope calculations, but a package like that could raise more than $450 billion in 1984 dollars, pretty close to a target some observers feel is reasonable: reducing half of the deficit with tax increases and half with spending cuts. In fact, the high-income surtax mechanism is already almost in place. The "minimum tax" on individuals adopted in 1969 and "reformed" in 1982 requires married couples whose real income (taxable income, plus excluded preference items) exceeds $40,000 (and singles earning more than $30,000) to pay a minimum tax of 20 percent.

This minimum tax was imposed because the loopholes were being so jealously guarded by the industries whose lives depended on them, that the only method of attack was by indirection. The Congress was unable to repeal many of the tax preferences. But it was politically indefensible to say rich people shouldn't pay some minimum portion of their economic income in taxes. Once a "tax preference" was included in the tax base, the sole issue became how high a "minimum tax" the rich should pay on this newly defined "income."

Some observers even predicted that the minimum tax would eventually replace the regular tax. The same prediction could be made of a low-level sales tax. A low-level sales tax could pay for an increase in the standard reduction that would remove millions of middle-income taxpayers from the burden of annual filing of tax returns. Then, with each increase in the sales tax, more individuals could be exempted from the income tax. But don't hold your breath.

THE LOOPHOLE MONGERS

Loopholes and tax preferences don't just "happen." A few may start without much attention—like the deduction for home mortgage interest—but they don't survive the relentless assault of the tax "purists" in the Treasury Department and populist tax reformers in Congress unless they can develop a powerful constituency.

There are some who believe that even without a major tax reform bill, Congress will inexorably remove more and more of the special tax incentives placed in the law in the past 70 years. During the 1960s and 1970s, there were several attempts at tax reform. But the motivation was seldom the need to raise revenue. Rather, tax reforms were adopted to respond to popular perceptions of unfairness. For example, after newspaper articles were published disclosing that many millionaires often paid no income taxes, the Congress responded with a "minimum tax" plan. But the only real need was to stop the articles, not to raise revenue.

Inflation was pushing taxpayers into higher brackets each year, and filling the government's coffers with more than enough money to support tax legislation that would not only cut back on the most obnoxious loopholes, but would also lower taxes across the board. During these "fat" years financed by "bracket creep," there was even enough money to create a few new tax preferences each year.

The income tax rate reductions of the Reagan tax cut in 1981 and the enactment of tax-bracket indexing changed the climate dramatically. With a perceived need to raise taxes in 1982 and 1984—and no automatic bracket creep to fall back on—closing loopholes was no longer a gentlemanly pursuit of abstract notions of fairness. Instead, in the "lean years" after 1981, the process of tax reform became a war between the general interest in keeping tax rates low and the special interests concerned with protecting the implicit subsidies embedded in the tax code for over 70 years.

Even the vocabulary of tax reform changed in the combat zone. Industry lobbyists before the House Ways and Means Committee and Senate Finance Committee not only defended their *explicit* tax subsidies (like accelerated depreciation for low-income housing or expensing of intangible oil-drilling costs) but also spoke up for the preservation of truly *unintended* loopholes. In the latter case, the lobbyists argued that their industry was being asked to make too great a contribution to tax reform. The issue was not whether an abusive tax shelter had been intended by the Congress, but whether outlawing the gimmicks discovered by inventive tax lawyers would hurt the housing industry, oil industry, banking community, or another sector whose cash flow was "critical to continued economic recovery."

The "effective tax rates" of different industries became a buzzword. And for those industries that were embarrassed by their low effective tax rates, lobbyists distributed poop sheets comparing the relative "contribution" of their clients to the gross amount of revenue raised by the 1982 or 1984 tax bill (without any mention that the bottom line still left them with massive tax subsidies).

During the 1984 tax debate, real estate interests were actually *threatened* with tax-exemption. That's right. It was carefully explained that if all the income from leased real estate was completely exempted from taxes (both rental income and capital gains) and all associated deductions for interest and depreciation were disallowed, the Treasury Department would actually *raise* billions of dollars each year. In other words, real estate investors were enjoying the kind of welfare system that had once been proposed for the poor—a negative income tax!

DIVIDING THE SPOILS

Most fundamental tax reform proposals like the flat, FAIR, FAST, and Treasury Department tax plans propose to institutionalize the trend of the 1980s toward reducing tax subsidies (base broadening) and flattening and lowering the tax rates. Fundamental tax reform poses a special threat to the "loophole mongers" who divide the spoils of the tax system with individuals and corporations who use tax sheltered investments to make their *taxable* income much lower than their real *economic* income.

Almost every tax subsidy operates as a "bribe" paid to an individual to spend, lend, or invest money with an enterprise that has been blessed by Congress with a deduction or exclusion that bears no relationship to the economic reality of measuring the true income of an individual or the profits of a corporation. The "spoils" of the tax system are then divided between a "bribe" for the individual taxpayer and a subsidy for the intended beneficiary. The beneficiary may be a university library (charitable contribution deduction), a low-income housing developer (depreciation), an oil wildcatter (intangible drilling costs), or a state government (tax-free municipal bonds).

Municipal bonds illustrate the varying ways tax subsidies can be divided between the intended beneficiary (the city or state government) and the investor who is "bribed" to purchase a lower yielding municipal bond. Long-term tax-exempt bonds may pay 10 percent interest to an individual investor, as opposed to 14 percent for a taxable bond. But for a taxpayer in the 50 percent tax bracket, the "bribe" makes it worthwhile. A tax-free return of 10 percent is much better than a return of 7 percent (what's left of the 14 percent yield after taxes). On a $1,000 bond, the government loses $70 of taxes and the city saves $40 in interest costs. The other $30 is the "bribe" paid to the investor. His after tax return is $30 dollars better than breaking even on a taxable bond.

In contrast, some short-term tax-exempt bonds pay 6 percent when equivalent taxable bonds are yielding 10 percent. Here the "bribe" to the investor is much less, and the benefit to the city or state can be just as great. The top-bracket investor would be only $10 better off with a $60 tax-free yield than a $50 yield after taxes. But the city has saved the same $40 in interest costs. The point is that sometimes tax subsidies go principally to the intended beneficiary—like the city issuing the short-term bond. Other times, almost as much is given away in "incentives" to the investor.

There is no annual review of the "efficiency" of these tax subsidies since they are permanently in the tax laws—until inertia is overcome and someone tries to remove them.

WATCHING THE RHETORIC

Regardless of how efficiently the spoils are divided, the loophole mongers are jealous of their privileges—and fearful that direct subsidies would simply not be forthcoming if their tax subsidies were removed by "tax reform." And depending on the relative size of taxpayer incentives, compared to the tax subsidy actually enjoyed by tax-favored industries, an industry's Washington lobbyists can be as helpful to high-income taxpayers seeking to reduce their personal taxes as they are to their paying clients.

Any proposal to simplify the income tax, replace it with a consumption tax, or alter the relative tax burden of the rich, poor, or middle class, must take into account the impact on the loophole mongers. Their very survival may depend on maintaining a tax deduction or exemption that may be relatively inconsequential, even to the individual taxpayers who take advantage of it.

Most individuals feel that lower tax rates would be beneficial for almost everyone. But we already saw (back in Chapter 6) how the real estate industry felt threatened by a simple, across-the-board rate reduction. Although the National Association of Realtors hasn't opposed tax rate reductions, they *have* insisted that tax rate reductions be accompanied by new subsidy programs to compensate for the reduced impact of the mortgage interest deduction.

And see if you can guess who engaged in the following "point and counterpoint" on the importance of the charitable contribution deduction to educational institutions.

> *Point:* "It would be depressing in the extreme if taxes were the only or even the dominant influence on individual decisions to give, and there is no evidence that that is the case."

> *Counterpoint:* ". . . complete elimination of the charitable deduction in 1970 (with the marginal rates then in effect) would have reduced total charitable contributions on the part of those who itemize deductions by 26 percent and would have cut gifts to educational institutions by almost half.

Need a hint? You'll probably never guess that both statements were made to the Senate Finance Committee on the same day by Princeton University President (and economics professor) William G. Bowen, on behalf of 11 top educational lobbies.

The two statements are not *really* contradictory, you see. As the professor of economics went on to explain, the tax deduction mainly affects the *size* of the contributions. Not the total number of contributions. And you don't need to be an economics professor to know that $1,000 gifts are better than $10 gifts (holding all other variables constant, of course).

Advanced degrees in economics can, of course, provide some helpful nuances. For example, even without eliminating the charitable deduction, merely lowering the top tax rates on wealthy individuals could hurt the "college of your choice." (This was the same point made by the president of the Realtors' Association.) Professor Bowen went on to explain that merely lowering the top tax rates would have an adverse impact on contributions to higher education "even greater than the impact on charitable giving generally because of the disproportionate dependence of higher education on donors who are more sensitive to the net cost of giving."

As you can see, talk of fundamental tax reform is driving brilliant academics and perceptive captains of industry to some awkward defenses of their tax privileges.

But, of course, there are some very good, sound arguments for keeping tax rates high and preserving charitable contribution deductions, tax-exempt bonds, and other tax shelters. After all, how do you think we got the tax system we have now?

Appendix A:
Who Pays Taxes?

Exhibits A.1 and A.2 provide basic information on the distribution of income and tax liabilities among different income groups. The statistics on average tax rates in the two exhibits differ primarily because the first (Exhibit A.1) uses a more comprehensive definition of real economic income. The second uses a measure of income that is broader than shown on tax returns, but still excludes some significant items (such as interest on municipal bonds).

The average tax rate is a simple fraction obtained by dividing taxes paid by income. The marginal tax rates shown in Exhibit A.1 are the average rates at which an additional dollar of income would be taxed for each income class.

Exhibit A.1. Treasury Department estimates of average tax rates and marginal tax rates for families at different levels of economic income in 1986.

Income class	Average tax rate	Marginal tax rate
Under $10,000	1.4%	4.2%
$10,000 to $15,000	3.2%	9.4%
$15,000 to $20,000	4.6%	12.4%
$20,000 to $30,000	6.2%	16.0%
$30,000 to $50,000	7.8%	20.9%
$50,000 to $100,000	9.4%	27.6%
$100,000 to $200,000	13.2%	37.5%
$200,000 and over	20.9%	46.1%

Source: *Treasury Department Report to the President,* Vol. 1, p. 47. November 24, 1984. Office of the Secretary, Department of the Treasury.

Exhibit A.2. Expanded income, tax liability, and average tax rate by size of expanded income. Computed using 1981 income levels, assuming law applicable in 1985. (Preliminary estimates by the Staff of the Congressional Joint Committee on Taxation.)

Expanded income[1] (thousands)	Expanded income (millions)	Tax liability[2] 1985 (millions)	Average tax rate (tax liability divided by income; percent)
Below $5	$30,451	$300	—10
$5 to $10	131,126	4,147	3.2
$10 to $15	175,282	12,780	7.3
$15 to $20	190,239	17,090	9.0
$20 to $30	400,468	42,230	10.5
$30 to $50	502,886	65,205	13.0
$50 to $100	232,062	39,192	16.9
$100 to $200	78,175	17,527	22.4
$200 above	83,626	20,706	24.8
Total	1,824,314	218,576	12.0

[1]Expanded income equals gross income plus excluded capital gains and various tax preference items less investment interest to the extent of investment income. The expanded income statistics include all returns and exclude non-filers.

[2]This is preliminary data. Tax liabilities include the refundable portion of the earned income credit, but do not include changes made to individual retirement accounts and ACRS by the Tax Equity and Fiscal Responsibility Act of 1982 for which tax return data are not available.

Source: *Joint Committee Print*, JCS-31-84, August 6, 1984. U.S. Government Printing Office.

Appendix B:
Who Doesn't Pay Taxes?

Exhibits B.1 and B.2 contain official IRS estimates of the extent of taxpayer noncompliance with existing tax laws. Exhibit B.1 provides an estimate of the amount of lost tax revenues (the "tax gap") attributable to various kinds of noncompliance. In addition to individual failures to report income, the tax gap is broken down into the amounts attributable to corporate noncompliance, individual nonfilers (individuals who completely fail to file tax returns), overstated deductions, and unreported income from certain illegal businesses.

Exhibit B.1. Income tax gap, 1973-1981. (In billions of dollars.)

	1973	1976	1979	1981
Legal sector tax gap, total	28.8	39.2	62.3	81.5
Corporation tax gap, total	3.5	4.6	6.4	6.2
Individual tax gap, total	25.3	34.6	55.9	75.3
Individual income tax liability reporting gap, total	23.8	32.2	50.6	68.5
Nonfilers' income tax liability (Net of prepayments and credits)	0.9	1.4	2.0	2.9
Filers' income tax liability:	22.9	30.8	48.6	65.6
Unreported income	17.3	24.2	38.4	52.2
Overstated business expenses . . .	2.1	3.4	4.7	6.3
Overstated personal deductions[1]	3.4	3.0	5.0	6.6
Net math error	0.1	0.2	0.5	0.5
Individual income tax remittance gap, total	1.5	2.4	5.3	6.8
Employer underdeposit of withholding[2]	1.1	0.9	1.8	2.4
Individual balance due after remittance	0.4	1.5	3.5	4.4
Illegal sector tax gap (partial)[3]	2.1	3.4	6.3	9.0
	(0.8)	(1.3)	(2.2)	(3.2)

[1]Includes itemized deductions, personal exemptions, and statutory adjustments.

[2]Also includes a small amount for underreported withholding by employees and a small negative amount for underclaimed withholding by individuals.

[3]Includes income from illegal drugs, illegal gambling, and prostitution only. Figures in parentheses are standard errors.

Source: IRS Statement on Tax Compliance before the Senate Finance Committee, June 23, 1983.

Exhibit B.2 provides an estimate of the actual dollar amounts of unreported individual income from activities other than illegal businesses.

Exhibit B.2. Unreported legal-source income of individual filers and nonfilers, 1973-1981. (In millions of dollars.)

	1973	1976	1979	1981
Wages and salaries	33,304	46,274	71,076	94,581
Dividends	1,920	3,638	5,528	8,747
Interest	4,440	6,763	11,548	20,479
Capital gains	5,015	9,935	16,283	17,727
Nonfarm proprietor income and small business corporations income (except informal supplier income).............	23,906	32,565	47,246	58,400
Farm proprietor income	5,742	4,542	7,832	9,547
Informal supplier income	10,346	12,721	16,995	17,080
Pensions and annuities	3,123	4,067	6,258	8,799
Rents	1,335	2,390	2,711	3,049
Royalties	312	1,088	1,672	2,770
Estate and trust income	487	695	1,140	1,330
State income tax refunds, alimony, and other income	3,990	6,857	6,260	7,166
Total income[1]	93,919	131,535	194,548	249,675

[1]Total may not equal sum of components due to rounding.

Source: IRS Statement on Tax Compliance before the Senate Finance Committee, June 23, 1983.

Appendix C:
Tax Expenditures

The concept of a "tax expenditure" is explained on page 20. Briefly, a tax expenditure is a special provision intended to "forgive" or reduce a tax liability as a reward or incentive for a certain kind of behavior. Exhibit C.1 provides an estimate of the amount of lost tax revenue attributable to various special deductions, exclusions, or credits that have been classified as tax expenditures. The estimates are categorized by their budget function, much as if they were direct federal outlays. They are also categorized as either individuals or corporate tax expenditures, depending on the extent to which individuals or corporations utilize these provisions to reduce their tax liabilities.

Exhibit C.1. Tax expenditure estimates by budget function, fiscal year 1985[1]. (In millions of dollars.)

Function	Corporations 1985	Individuals 1985
National defense:		
Exclusion of benefits and allowances to Armed Forces personnel	—	2,030
Exclusion of military disability pensions	—	125
International affairs:		
Exclusion of income earned abroad by United States citizens	—	1,405
Deferral of income of domestic international sales corporation (DISC)	1,195	—
Deferral of income of controlled foreign corporations	375	—
General science, space, and technology:		
Expensing of research and development expenditures	3,100	125
Credit for increasing research activities	1,740	20
Suspension of regulations relating to allocation under Section 861 of research and experimental expenditures	(4)	—
Energy:		
Expensing of exploration and development costs		

Function	Corporations 1985	Individuals 1985
Oil and gas	1,075	1,135
Other fuels	35	—
Excess of percentage over cost depletion:		
Oil and gas	335	805
Other fuels	355	15
Capital gains treatment of royalties from coal	40	140
Alternative fuel production credit	25	—
Alcohol fuel credit[2]	5	—
Exclusion of interest on state and local government industrial development bonds for energy production facilities	120	60
Residential energy credits:		
Supply incentives	—	470
Conservation incentives	—	305
Alternative, conservation, and new technology energy property credits:		
Supply incentives	175	5
Conservation incentives	15	(4)
Energy credit for intercity buses	5	—
Natural resources and environment:		
Expensing of exploration and development costs, nonfuel minerals	65	(4)
Excess of percentage over cost depletion, nonfuel minerals	365	15
Capital gains treatment of certain timber income	490	175
Investment credit and 7-year amortization for reforestation expenditures	(2)	10
Capital gains treatment of iron ore	10	10
Exclusion of interest on state and local government bonds for pollution control and sewage and waste disposal facilities	1,285	635
Tax incentives for preservation of historic structures	130	250
Agriculture:		
Expensing of certain capital outlays	70	400
Capital gains treatment of certain income	35	640
Deductibility of patronage dividends and certain other items of cooperatives	1,010	-410

Function	Corporations 1985	Individuals 1985
Commerce and housing:		
Dividend exclusion	—	455
Reinvestment of dividends in stock of public utilities	—	450
Net interest exclusion	—	1,025
Exclusion of interest on state and local government industrial development bonds	3,125	740
Exemption of credit union income	185	—
Exclusion of interest on life insurance savings	—	5,180
Excess bad debt reserves of financial institutions	795	—
Deductibility of nonmortgage interest in excess of investment income	—	6,950
Deductibility of mortgage interest on owner-occupied homes	—	25,460
Deductibility of property tax on owner-occupied homes	—	9,640
Exclusion of interest on state and local government housing bonds for owner-occupied housing	1,260	560
Exclusion of interest on state and local government housing bonds for rental housing	920	445
Deferral of capital gains on home sales	—	5,625
Exclusion of capital gains on home sales for persons age 55 and over	—	1,875
Accelerated depreciation on rental housing	165	710
Accelerated depreciation on buildings other than rental housing	210	165
Accelerated depreciation on equipment other than leased property	18,925	2,870
Finance leasing	435	—
Amortization of business start-up costs	25	230
Capital gains other than agriculture, timber, iron ore and coal	2,515	18,485
Capital gains at death	—	4,355
Reduced rates on the first $100,000 of corporate income	7,580	—
Investment credit, other than ESOPs, rehabilitation of structures, reforestation, leasing, and energy property	29,355	5,445

Function	Corporations 1985	Individuals 1985
Transportation:		
Amortization of motor carrier operating rights	50	5
Deferral of tax on shipping companies	45	—
Exclusion of interest on state and local government mass transit bonds	85	40
Community and regional development:		
Five-year amortization for housing rehabilitation	25	35
Investment credit for rehabilitation of structures other than historic structures	185	160
Private airport, dock, and convention facility bonds	350	175
Education, training, employment, and social services:		
Exclusion of scholarship and fellowship income	—	570
Exclusion of interest on state and local government student loan bonds	355	170
Exclusion of interest on state and local government bonds for private educational facilities	315	150
Parental personal exemption for students age 19 or over	—	1,020
Exclusion of employee meals and lodging (other than military)	—	795
Exclusion of contributions to prepaid legal services plans	—	15
Exclusion for employer provided child care	—	70
Tax credit for ESOPs	2,295	—
Deductibility for charitable contributions for education	360	810
Deductibility for charitable contributions, other than education and health	445	11,055
Credit for child and dependent care expenses	—	1,905
Targeted jobs credit	470	35
Deduction for two-earner married couples	—	6,350

Function	Corporations 1985	Individuals 1985
Deduction for adoption expenses	—	10
Cafeteria plans	—	75
Health:		
Exclusion of employer contributions for medical insurance premiums and medical care	—	20,165
Deductibility of medical expenses	—	3,410
Exclusion of interest on state and local government bonds for hospital facilities	1,025	490
Deductibility of charitable contributions for health	—	1,620
Tax credit for orphan drug research	15	—
Income security:		
Exclusion of untaxed social security benefits:		
Disability insurance benefits	—	1,105
OASI benefits for retired workers	—	12,975
Benefits for dependents and survivors	—	3,765
Exclusion of untaxed railroad retirement system benefits	—	450
Exclusion of workers' compensation benefits	—	2,215
Exclusion of special benefits for disabled coal miners	—	155
Exclusion of untaxed unemployment insurance benefits	—	1,800
Exclusion of public assistance benefits	—	510
Exclusion of disability pay[3]	—	—
Net exclusion of pension contributions and earnings:		
Employer plans	—	52,670
Plans for self-employed	—	1,530
Individual retirement plans	—	9,840
Exclusion of other employee benefits:		
Premiums on group term life insurance	—	2,380
Premiums on accident and disability insurance	—	125
Additional exemption for the blind	—	30

Additional exemption for elderly	—	2,450
Elderly and disabled credit[3]	—	210
Deductibility of casualty and theft losses	·	415
Earned income credit[5]	—	285
Veterans benefits and services:		
Exclusion of veterans disability compensation	—	1,855
Exclusion of veterans pensions	—	340
General government:		
Credits and deductions for political contributions	—	220
General purpose fiscal assistance:		
Exclusion of interest on general purpose state and local government debt	8,740	4,255
Deductibility of nonbusiness state and local government taxes other than on owner-occupied homes	—	21,635
Tax credit for corporations receiving income from doing business in U.S. possessions	1,135	—
Exclusion of possessions source income	1,440	—
Interest:		
Deferral of interest on savings bonds	—	770

Footnotes:

[1] All estimates are based on the tax law enacted through December 31, 1983.

[2] In addition, the $0.05/gallon exemption from the excise tax for alcohol fuel results in a reduction in excise tax receipts, net of income tax effect, of approximately $145 million for 1984, $150 million for 1985, $160 million for 1986, $175 million for 1987, $185 million for 1988 and $60 million for 1989.

[3] The disability pay exclusion was replaced with a credit in the 1983 Social Security Act.

[4] Less than $5 million.

[5] The figures in the table indicate the effect of the earned income credit on receipts. The increase in outlays is $1,070 million in 1984, $990 million in 1985, $955 million in 1986, $935 million in 1987, $880 million in 1988, and $755 million in 1989.

Source: Joint Committee Print, JCS-39-84, November 9, 1984. U.S. Government Printing Office.

Appendix D:
Effective Tax Rates of Different Industries

Exhibit D.1 summarizes a study of the effective tax rates of 218 large companies selected from the *Fortune* 500 Industrials and the *Fortune* Service 500. The study was performed in 1984 by the staff of the Congressional Joint Committee on Taxation at the request of Congressman Don J. Pease (D., Ohio) and Congressman Byron Dorgan (D., North Dakota).

The table reports the current income and current tax expense attributable to each industry group's domestic and foreign activities, as reported in public financial statements. It also reports on the worldwide income and worldwide tax expense of the companies studied. The effective tax rate computation is obtained by dividing current tax expense by current income.

Exhibit D.1. Comparison of corporate effective tax rates by industry, 1983.

	Thousands of dollars						Tax rate (percent)		
	U.S. income before tax	Foreign income before tax	World-wide income before tax	Current U.S. tax expense	Current foreign tax expense	Current world-wide tax expense	U.S. tax rate on U.S. income	Foreign tax rate on foreign income	World-wide tax rate on world-wide income
Aerospace	3,287,418	373,107	3,660,525	459,337	201,611	660,948	14.0	54.0	18.1
Beverages	1,688,161	577,327	2,265,488	316,120	301,673	617,793	18.7	52.3	27.3
Broadcasting ...	1,081,109	209,552	1,290,661	199,818	79,957	279,775	18.5	38.2	21.7
Chemicals	1,164,100	3,416,300	4,580,400	(11,100)	2,433,900	2,422,800	(1.0)	71.2	52.9
Computers and office equipment ...	6,842,475	4,972,408	11,814,883	1,796,917	2,702,044	4,498,961	26.3	54.3	38.1
Construction...	59,386	195,035	254,421	429	74,134	74,563	.7	38.0	29.3
Electronics and appliances	3,952,658	1,482,062	5,434,720	290,863	598,646	889,509	7.4	40.4	16.4
Financial institutions ...	2,862,830	3,460,057	6,322,887	182,040	1,354,023	1,536,063	6.4	39.1	24.3
Food processors ...	3,810,004	1,309,634	5,119,638	987,286	511,118	1,498,404	25.9	39.0	29.3
Glass and concrete......	605,401	180,435	785,836	105,754	85,725	191,479	17.5	47.5	24.4
Instruments ...	2,256,478	659,639	2,916,117	739,600	330,291	1,069,891	32.8	50.1	36.7
Insurance	1,755,975	48,800	1,804,775	174,398	58,491	232,889	9.9	(1)	12.9
Investment companies	979,855	680,650	1,660,505	91,478	137,383	228,861	9.3	20.2	13.8

Industry								
Metal manufacturing	(1,341,203)	16,600	(1,324,603)	25,396	40,300	65,696	(1)	(1)	(1)
Metal products	286,113	318,686	604,799	43,296	133,960	177,256	15.1	42.0	29.3
Mining	(485,812)	145,328	(340,484)	(18,861)	70,961	52,100	(1)	48.8	(1)
Motor vehicles	5,759,186	1,281,402	7,040,588	202,308	527,330	729,638	3.5	41.2	10.4
Paper and wood products	759,318	118,263	877,581	(3,846)	66,917	63,071	(.5)	56.6	7.2
Petroleum	19,255,863	22,171,133	41,426,996	4,094,087	13,303,397	17,397,484	21.3	60.0	42.0
Pharmaceuticals	2,301,842	1,549,400	3,851,242	626,033	608,331	1,234,364	27.2	39.3	32.1
Retailing	5,067,076	288,367	5,355,443	1,015,447	125,630	1,141,077	20.0	43.6	21.3
Rubber	618,089	283,821	901,910	121,366	194,260	315,626	19.6	68.4	35.0
Soaps and cosmetics	2,027,044	513,380	2,540,424	720,699	266,857	987,556	35.6	52.0	38.9
Telecommunications	1-,072,260	127,117	11,199,377	530,913	96,978	627,891	4.8	(1)	5.6
Tobacco	3,083,254	539,760	3,623,014	1,041,548	150,751	1,192,299	33.8	27.9	32.9
Transportation: Airlines	(272,024)	169,123	(102,901)	(58,828)	4,464	(54,364)	(1)	2.6	(1)
Railroads	2,164,765	. . . .	2,164,765	71,899	. . . .	71,899	3.3	. . . . .	3.3
Trucking	1,283,557	7,824	1,291,381	442,768	4,278	447,046	34.5	54.7	34.6
Utilities (electric and gas)	7,158,433	. . . .	7,158,433	505,298	. . . .	505,298	7.1	. . . . .	7.1
Wholesalers	947,776	9,200	956,976	329,472	13,806	343,278	34.8	(1)	35.9
Average, All Companies	90,031,387	45,104,410	135,135,797	15,021,935	24,477,216	39,499,151	16.7	54.3	29.2

[1]Rate not computed.

Source: *Joint Committee Print*, JCS-40-84, November 28, 1984. U.S. Government Printing Office.

Appendix E:
Summary Comparison of Different Tax Reform Proposals

Exhibit E.1, prepared by the U.S. Department of the Treasury, compares the provisions of the Treasury Department's tax reform proposal with several tax reform bills introduced by Members of Congress.

Exhibit E.1. Comparison of Treasury Proposal with Congressional tax reform bills.

	Treasury Department (TD)	Bradley-Gephardt (B-G)	Kemp-Kasten (K-K)	Roth-Moore (R-M)	Nickles-Siljander (N-S)	De Concini-Shelby (D-S)
I. Individual income taxes						
A. *Rate Reduction*	3 rates: 15%, 25% 35%[1]	3 rates: 14%, 26% 30%[2]	25% of taxable income. Exclusion for 20% of wages in FICA tax base[3]	4 rates: 12, 20, 30, & 34 on taxable income[4]	10% of taxable income[5]	19% of compensation[6]
B. *Fairness for Families*						
1. Zero bracket amount.[7]						
a. Single returns	$ 2,800	$ 3,000	$ 2,700	$ 2,400	$ 0	$ 4,100
b. Married (joint return)	3,800	6,000	3,500	3,550	0	6,700
c. Married (separate return)	1,900	3,000	1,750	1,775	0	4,100
d. Head of household return	3,500	3,000	2,700	2,400	0	6,000
2. Personal exemptions[8]						
a. Taxpayer	$ 2,000	$ 1,600[9]	$ 2,000	$ 1,050	$ 2,000	0
b. Dependent (each)	2,000	1,000	2,000[10]	1,050	2,000[11]	$ 810
c. Blind and elderly (each)	0	1,000	2,000	0	0	0
3. Tax-free amount excluding the earned income credit (1986 levels)						
a. Single returns	$ 4,800	$ 4,600	$ 5,130[12]	$ 3,610	$ 2,090	$ 4,470
b. Joint returns						
Family of 2	7,800	9,200	8,180[12]	5,920	4,180	7,310
Family of 4	11,800	11,200	12,540[12]	8,120	8,360	9,070
Family of 6	15,800	13,200	16,900[12]	10,320	12,540	10,830
c. Head of household returns						
Family of 2	7,500	5,800	7,310[12]	4,710	4,180	7,430
Family of 4	11,500	7,800	11,670[12]	6,910	8,360	9,190
Family of 6	14,500	9,800	16,030[12]	9,110	12,540	10,950

(TD)	(B-G)	(K-K)	(R-M)	(N-S)	(D-S)
4. Provide a single credit for the elderly, blind, and disabled to replace the exemptions for the elderly and the blind.	Repeals credit for elderly and disabled	Repeals credit for elderly and disabled	Repeals credit for elderly and disabled	Repeals credit for elderly and disabled	Repeals credit for elderly and disabled
5. Repeal deduction for two-earner married couples.	Yes	Yes	Yes	Yes	Yes
6. Indexation of zero bracket amount, personal and dependents exemptions, and dollar amounts of earned income credit (EITC).	No	Yes. Also reduces EITC.	Yes. Also increases EITC.	Indexation. Repeals EITC.	Yes. Repeals EITC.
7. Replace child and dependent care credit with a deduction from gross income with cap on allowable expenses.	Yes[13]	Repeals credit	Repeals credit	Repeals credit	Repeals credit

C. *Fair and Neutral Taxation*

[1.] Excluded Sources of Income

(TD)	(B-G)	(K-K)	(R-M)	(N-S)	(D-S)
1. Repeal exclusion of health insurance above a cap.	Limits exclusion[14]	No	Limits exclusion[14]	Repeals exclusion	No[15]
2. Repeal exclusion of group term life insurance.	Yes[16]	No	No[16]	No	No[15]
3. Repeal exclusion of employer-provided death benefits.	No	No	Yes	Yes	No[15]
4. Repeal exclusion of dependent care services or reimbursement.	Yes	No	Yes	Yes	No[15]
5. Repeal special treatment of cafeteria plans.	Yes	No	Yes	Yes	No[15]

	1	2	3	4	5	6
6. Repeal exemption of voluntary employee's beneficiary associations and trusts for supplemental unemployment compensation and black lung disability.	No	No	No	No	No	No
7. Repeal special provisions regarding incentive stock options.	No[15]	No	No	No	No	No
8. Repeal exclusion of military compensation with offsetting adjustments in military pay; mustering out pay.	No[15]	Limited repeal of military tax-free allowances	Limited repeal of military tax-free allowances	No[15]	No	No
9. Repeal exclusion of rental allowances or rental value of minister's home.	No[15]	Yes	Yes	No	No	No
[2.] Wage replacement payments						
1. Repeal tax-exempt threshold for unemployment insurance compensation.	No	Yes	Yes	Yes	Yes	Yes
2. Repeal tax exemption of workers' compensation payments, black lung, and certain veterans' disability payments, but make such income eligible for the credit for the blind, elderly, and disabled.	Repeals exemption and credit.	Exempts disability payments. Repeals credit.	Repeals exemption for certain disability payments. Repeals credit.	Repeals exemption for certain disability payments. Repeals credit.	No — Repeals credit.	No
[3.] Other excluded sources of income						
1. Repeal exclusion of scholarships and fellowships in excess of tuition.	No	No	Yes	Yes	Yes	Yes
2. Repeal exclusion of awards and prizes.	Yes	No	No	No	No	No

(TD)	(B-G)	(K-K)	(R-M)	(N-S)	(D-S)
[4.] Preferred uses of income					
a. Repeal itemized deduction for state and local taxes:					
1. State and local real property taxes	No[13]	No	Yes	No	Yes
2. State and local personal property taxes	Yes	No	Yes	No	Yes
3. State and local income taxes	No[13]	Yes	Yes	No	Yes
4. State and local general sales taxes	Yes	No	Yes	No	Yes[17]
b. Repeal the above-the-line deduction for charitable contributions.	No[13]	No	No	No	Yes[17]
c. Limit deductions for charitable contributions to those in excess of 2 percent of gross income.	No[13]	No	No	No	No[17]
d. Limit deduction of charitable contributions of appreciated property to the indexed basis.	No	No	No	No	No[17]
e. Repeal 50% and 30% limits on individual contributions.	No	No	No	No	No[17]
f. Repeal 10% limit on corporate contributions (but retain 5% limit in certain cases).	Amends deduction[18]	No	No	No	No[17]
D. *Tax Abuses*					
1. Business Deductions for Personal Expenses					

a. Deny all entertainment expenses including club dues and tickets to public events except for business meals furnished in a clear business setting. Limit deductions for business meals on a per-meal per-person basis.	No	No	No	No[19]
b. Limit deductions for meals and lodging away from home in excess of 200% of the federal per diem. When travel lasts longer than 30 days in one city, limit deductions to 150 percent of the federal per diem (and disallow incidental expenses).	No	No	No	No[19]
c. Establish bright-line rules to separate indefinite and temporary assignments at 1 year.	No	No	No	No[19]
d. Extend foreign travel rules for allocation of expenses between personal and business expenses to all travel.	No	No	No	No[19]
e. Deny all deductions for travel as a form of education.	No	No	No	No[19]
f. Deny deductions for seminars held aboard cruise ships.	No	No	No	No[19]
g. Deny any deductions for travel by ocean liner, cruise ship, or other form of luxury water transportation above cost of otherwise available business transportation with medical exception.	No	No	No	No[19]

(TD)	(B-G)	(K-K)	(R-M)	(N-S)	(D-S)
2. Income Shifting					
a. Revise grantor trust rules to eliminate shifting of income to lower rate beneficiaries through trusts in which the creator retains an interest.	No	No	No	No	No[21]
b. During lifetime of creator, tax trust at creator's marginal rate and allow deductions only for nondiscretionary distributions and set-asides. After creator's death, tax all undistributed trust or estate income at top marginal rate.	No	No	No	No	No[21]
c. Tax unearned income of children under 14 at the parent's tax rate (to the extent that such income exceeds the child's personal exemption).	No	No	No	No	No[21]
d. Revise income taxation of trusts.	No[20]	No[20]	No	No	No
E. Further Simplification					
1. Nonfiling system, in which IRS would compute tax for many taxpayers.	No	No	No	No	No
2. Repeal individual minimum taxes.	Yes	No	Yes	Yes	Yes
3. Move miscellaneous deductions above the line, combine with employee business expenses and make subject to a floor.	No[13]	No	No	No	No
4. Repeal preferential treatment of capital gains.	Yes	Yes, for individuals.	Yes	No	Yes

5. Repeal political contribution credit.	Yes	Yes	Yes	Yes	Yes
6. Repeal presidential campaign checkoff.	No	No	No	No	Yes
7. Repeal deduction of adoption expenses for children with special needs, and replace with a direct expenditure program.	Repeals deduction only	No	Repeals deduction only	Repeals deduction only	Repeals deduction only
8. Disallow income averaging for taxpayers who were full-time students during the base period.	Repeals income averaging	Repeals income averaging	Repeals income averaging	No	Repeals income averaging
9. Repeal $100/$200 exclusion of dividend income.	Yes	Yes	Yes	Yes	Yes
F. Other Miscellaneous Reforms					
1. Increase limits on moving expenses.	No	No	No. Repeals deduction	No	No. Repeals deduction
2. Special rule for allowing deduction of some commuting expenses of workers who have no regular place of work.	No	No	No	No	No
II. Basic taxation of capital and business income tax					
A. Lower Corporate Tax Rate					
1. Reduce maximum corporate rate to 33%.	30%	30% above $50,000	Retains current law	Retains current law	19% of business taxable income
2. Repeal graduated corporate rate structure	Yes	No. 15% to $50,000	Retains current law	Retains current law	Yes
3. Repeal personal holding company tax.	Yes	Yes	No	No	Yes

B. Taxing Real Economic Income

(TD)	(B-G)	(K-K)	(R-M)	(N-S)	(D-S)
1. Index capital gains and tax as ordinary income.	No indexation: tax as ordinary income[23]	Indexation: Tax as ordinary income for individuals[24]	No indexation: Tax as ordinary income[25]	Retains current law.[26]	No indexation: Tax as ordinary income
2. Index depreciation for inflation and set depreciation allowances to approximate economic depreciation.	Modified ADR: no inflation adjustment	ACRS: no inflation adjustment	Current law for corps. Expensing for certain equipment for individuals.	Retains current law for corps. Repeals allowances for individuals.	Expensing
3. Repeal investment tax credit.	Yes	Yes	Retains for corps. only	Yes, except for corps.	Yes
4. Repeal collapsible corporation rules.	Yes	No	No	No	No
5. Allow expensing of the first $5,000 of depreciable business property but repeal legislative increases in that dollar limit.	No	No	No[27]	No	No
6. Allow indexed FIFO and repeal conformity requirement.	No	No	No	No	No
7. Index interest receipts and payments in excess of mortgage interest plus $5,000.	No	No	No	No	No

C. Retirement Savings.

(TD)	(B-G)	(K-K)	(R-M)	(N-S)	(D-S)
1. Raise IRA limits to $2,500.	No	No	No[28]	No	No
2. Make IRAs available to both employees and spouses working in the home.	No	No	No[28]	No	No

3. Subject all tax-favored retirement plans (TFRP's) to uniform distribution rules.	No	No	No	No	No[29]
a. Subject all preretirement distributions from TFRP's to a 20 percent premature distributions tax, generally, and 10 percent for tuition and first-home purchase.	No	No	No	No	No[29]
b. Subject all TFRP's to uniform minimum distribution rules.	No	No	No	No	No[29]
c. Repeal 10-year averaging for lump-sum distribution.	Yes	Yes	Yes	No	No[29]
d. Eliminate special recovery rules for qualified plan distributions.	No	No	No	No	No[29]
e. Repeal special treatment for distributions of employer securities.	No	No	No	No	No[29]
4. Simplify the deduction, contribution, and benefit limits for TFRP's.					
a. Repeal aggregate-based deduction limits for profit-sharing and stock bonus plans.	No	No	No	No	No[29]
b. Subject excess contributions to a 6 percent excise tax to recapture excessive tax benefits.	No	No	No	No	No[29]
c. Repeal combined plan limit for non-top-heavy plans.	No[30]	No	No	No	No[29]
d. Subject all retirement distributions in excess of $112,500 per year to a 10 percent excise tax.	No	No	No	No	No[29]

	(TD)	(B-G)	(K-K)	(R-M)	(N-S)	(D-S)
5. Miscellaneous changes.						
a. Extend deduction limits for TFRP's to ESOP's, and repeal the ESOP credit.		Repeals ESOP credit only.	Repeals ESOP credit only.	No	No	No[31]
b. Repeal "cash and deferred arrangements"		No	No	No	No	No[29]
c. Postpone deductions for interest on debt incurred to finance employee contributions to TFRP's until taxable distributions are made.		No	No	No	No	No[29]
D. *Neutrality Toward the Form of Business Organization*						
1. Reduce double taxation of distributed corporate equity income by allowing a 50 percent dividend deduction.		No	No	No	No	No[22]
2. Require that all partnerships with more than 35 partners be taxed as corporations.		No	No	No	No	No
III. Industry-specific subsidies, tax shelters, and other issues						
A. *General Issues of Income Measurement*						
1. Match expenses and receipts from multiperiod production.		No[32]	No[32]	No	No	No

	(1)	(2)	(3)	(4)
2. Restrict use of cash accounting method.	Yes: limited to farming (including timber)	Yes: limited to farming (including timber)	No	No
3. Limit bad debt deductions to actual loan losses.	No	No	No	No
4. Disallow installment sales treatment when receivables are pledged.	No	No	No	No
5. Repeal corporate minimum tax.	Yes	No	No	Yes
B. Subsidies for Specific Industries				
1. Special rules for energy and natural resource industries.				
a. Repeal windfall profit tax.	No	No	No	No
b. Repeal percentage depletion; replace with cost depletion adjusted for inflation.	Yes: replaces with depreciation	Yes: replaces with depreciation	Repeals, except for corps.	No[33]
c. Repeal expensing of intangible drilling costs.	Yes	Yes	Repeals, except for corps.	No[33]
d. Repeal expensing of qualified tertiary injectant expenses.	Yes	No	Repeals, except for corps.	No[33]
e. Repeal expensing of hard mineral exploration and development costs.	Yes	Yes	Repeals, except for corps.	No[33]
f. Repeal special treatment of coal, oil, and timber royalty income.	Yes	Yes, except for corps.	No	Yes

(TD)	(B-G)	(K-K)	(R-M)	(N-S)	(D-S)
g. Repeal special rules for mining reclamation reserves.	No	No	No	Repeals, except for corps.	No[33]
h. Repeal nonconventional fuel production tax credit, alcohol fuel credit, and excise tax exemption.	Repeals credits	Repeals credits	Repeals credits, except for corps.	Repeals credits, except for corps.	Repeals credits
2. Special Rules of Financial Institutions					
a. Commercial banks and thrift institutions.					
1. Repeal special bad debt deductions for banks and thrift institutions.	No[34]	No[34]	No	No	No
2. Disallow 100% of interest incurred to carry tax-exempt bonds by depository institutions.	No	No	No	No	No
3. Repeal tax exemption of credit unions.	Yes	No	No	No	Yes
4. Repeal special carryover rules and special merger rules of thrift institutions.	No	No	No	No	No
b. Life insurance companies					
1. Limit life insurance reserve deductions to the increase in policyholders' cash surrender value.	No	No	No	No	No
2. Repeal special deduction of percentage of taxable income for life insurance companies.	No	No	No	No	No

	Col1	Col2	Col3	Col4
3. Repeal tax exemption for certain insurance companies.	No	No	No	No
c. Property and casualty (P&C) insurance companies				
1. Limit P&C reserves to the discounted present value of future liabilities.	No	No	No	No
2. Repeal mutual P&C insurance companies' deduction for additions to protection against loss accounts.	No	No	No	No
3. Limit deductibility of P&C policyholder dividends.	No	No	No	No
4. Repeal special tax exemption, rate reductions, and deductions of small mutual P&C insurance companies.	No	No	No	No
3. Insurance Investment Income				
a. Repeal exclusion of annual income on life insurance policies.	Yes	Yes	No	Yes[35]
b. Treat policyholder loans as coming first from any tax-exempt inside buildup.	No	No	No	No
c. Repeal exclusion of current annuity income.	Yes	Yes	No	Yes
4. State and Local Government Debt and Investment				
a. Repeal the tax exemption of private purpose tax-exempt bonds.	Yes	Yes	No	No
b. Tighten restrictions on tax arbitrage and advance refunding for tax-exempt bonds.	No	No	No	No

(TD)	(B-G)	(K-K)	(R-M)	(N-S)	(D-S)
5. Repeal special expensing and amortization rules.					
a. Repeal expensing of soil and water conservation expenditures, expenditures by farmers for fertilizer and for clearing fields.	Yes	Yes	No	Repeals, except for corps.	No
b. Repeal 5-year amortization of expenditures for rehabilitation of low income rental housing.	Yes	No	No	Repeals, except for corps.	No[33]
c. Repeal 5-year amortization of certified pollution control facilities.	Yes	No	No	Repeals, except for corps.	No[33]
d. Repeal 50-year amortization of railroad grading and tunnel bores.	No	No	No	Repeals except for corps.	No[33]
e. Repeal 5-year amortization of trademark expenses.	No	No	No	Repeals, except for corps.	No[33]
f. Repeal 84-month amortization of reforestation expenditures and 10 percent tax credit for such expenditures.	Yes	Yes	No	Repeals, except for corps.	No[33]
[6.] Other specific subsidies.					
a. Repeal rehabilitation tax credits.	Yes	Yes	Yes, except for corps.	Yes, except for corps.	Yes
b. Tighten rules for depreciating leasehold improvements.	No	Repeals	No	Repeals, except for corps.	No

c. Repeal special rules for returns of magazines and paperback books and for qualified discount coupons.	Yes	No	No	Repeals, except for corps.	No
d. Repeal exclusion relating to Merchant Marine Capital Construction Fund.	Yes	Yes	No	No	No
e. Rationalize credit for research and experimentation.	Repeals credit	Repeals credit	No	Repeals, except for corps.	Repeals credit
C. Further Curtailment of Tax Shelters					
1. Disallow most current deductions for schedule A interest in excess of sum of home mortgage interest, investment income, and income from limited partnerships and S corporations plus $5,000.	Allows deduction for home mortgage interest. Limits deduction for consumer interest.[36]	Allows deduction for home mortgage interest. Limits deduction for consumer interest.[37]	Allows deduction for home mortgage interest. Disallows deduction for consumer interest.	Retains current law.	Repeals interest deduction including home mortgage interest.
2. Extend limits on interest deduction where taxpayer is not at risk to real estate and equipment leasing.	No	No	No	No	No
D. International Issues[38]					
1. Change foreign tax credit limitation to a separate per-country limitation.	No	No	No	No	No
2. Modify rules defining source of income derived from sales of inventory-type property and intangible property.	No	No	No	No	No
3. Repeal the secondary dividend rule and replace with a branch profits tax.	No	No	No	No	No

(TD)	(B-G)	(K-K)	(R-M)	(N-S)	(D-S)
4. Repeal special preference for 80/20 corporations.	No	No	No	No	No
5. Clarify treatment of foreign exchange gains and losses.	No	No	No	No	No
6. Repeal posessions tax credit and replace with a phased out wage credit.	Repeals credit	No	No	No	Repeals credit
E. *Other Tax Issues*					
1. Transfer Taxation					
a. Unify estate and gift tax structure by grossing up the tax on gifts, and simplify rules for determining when a transfer is complete for gift tax purposes.	No	No	No	No	No
b. Simplify taxation of generation-skipping transfers, and modify credit for tax on prior transfers to a lower generation.	No	No	No	No	No
c. Impose a rule to prevent abuse of minority discounts.	No	No	No	No	No
d. Replace the rules governing payment of estate tax in installments with simplified rules based on estate liquidity, but make interest incurred by an estate nondeductible for estate tax purposes.	No	No	No	No	No

e. Reduce estate tax deduction for claims against an estate by the amount of income tax savings from payment of the expense.	No	No	No	No
f. Simplify state death tax credit and gift tax rate and credit by making it a flat percent of federal estate tax collected.	No	No	No	No
g. Repeal special tax rules for redemption of stock to pay death taxes.	No	No	No	No
h. Tighten rules regarding powers of appointment.	No	No	No	No
2. Penalties[39]				
a. Simplify information return penalties.	No	No	No	No
b. Repeal maximum limits on penalties.	No	No	No	No
c. Repeal failure to pay penalty with a cost-of-collection charge.	No	No	No	No
3. Expiring provisions				
a. Residential and certain business energy tax credits.	Repeals	Yes, except for corps.	Repeals	Repeals
b. Targeted jobs credit.	No stated proposal	No stated proposal	Repeals	Repeals
c. Expensing of expenditure to remove architectural barriers to the elderly and handicapped.	No stated proposal	No stated proposal	No stated proposal	Allows expensing[33]
d. Credit for testing orphan drugs.	Repeals	Repeals, except for corps.	Repeals, except for corps.	Repeals

	(TD)	(B-G)	(K-K)	(R-M)	(N-S)	(D-S)
e. Special treatment for dividend reinvestment in public utility stock.		Repeals	Repeals	Repeals	No stated proposal	Repeals
f. Exclusion of employer-provided legal services.		Repeals	Repeals	Repeals	Repeals	No stated proposal[15]
g. Exclusion of employer-provided education assistance.		Repeals	No stated proposal	Repeals	Repeals	No stated proposal[15]
h. Exclusion of employer provided vanpooling.		Repeals	Repeals	Repeals	Repeals	No stated proposal[15]

Source: Treasury Department Report to the President, Vol. 1, p. 169. Office of the Secretary, Department of the Treasury.

Footnotes

[1]For single returns the 15 percent rate would apply to taxable income above $2,800, the 25 percent rate to taxable income above $19,300, and the 35 percent rate to taxable income above $38,100. For joint returns the 15 percent rate would apply to taxable income above $3,800, the 25 percent rate to taxable income above $31,800, and the 35 percent rate to taxable income above $63,800. For head of household returns the 15 percent rate applies to taxable income above $3,500, the 25 percent rate to taxable income above $25,000 and the 35 percent rate to taxable income above $48,000.

[2]14% of taxable income; surtax of 12% on adjusted gross income (AGI) in excess of $40,000 or $25,000 for joint and single returns, respectively; surtax of 16% on AGI's in excess of $65,000 and $37,500 for joint and single returns, respectively. Heads of households would be treated like single individuals. The maximum rate would be 30%. Itemized deductions, personal exemptions, and the deductions for charitable contributions and child care expenses can only be used to calculate the tax subject to the 14 percent rate.

[3]If earned income is less than $15,000 for a married couple or $10,000 for a single person, 20% of total income may be excluded up to $10,000 or $15,000. Exclusion phases out at the rate of 12.5 cents per dollar of income in excess of the FICA wage base.

[4]These rates apply when the proposal is fully phased-in (1990 and thereafter).

[5] In N-S, taxable income of individuals excludes alimony, social security benefits, disability income, state and local bond income, railroad retirement benefits, and certain Federal retirement benefits.

[6] In D-S compensation is defined as cash wages. Non-cash fringe benefits are excluded from compensation.

[7] Estimated current law values for 1986 are $2,510, $3,710, $1,850, and $2,510 for single returns, joint returns, separate returns, and head of household returns, respectively. The ZBAs are at 1986 levels for TD, 1984 levels for KK, 1985 levels for R-M, 1984 levels for N-S, and 1983 levels for D-S.

[8] Estimated current law value for 1986 is $1,090. The exemptions are at 1986 levels for TD, 1984 levels for KK, 1985 levels for R-M, 1983 levels for D-S.

[9] B-G provides head of households an exemption of $1,800.

[10] K-K would disallow dependency exemptions for students over age 18.

[11] In N-S, dependency exemptions are limited to children, stepchildren under 18, full-time student dependents, and dependents with less that $2,000 of income.

[12] The amount shown represents the total of the zero bracket amount plus the personal exemptions. Taxpayers could also exclude 20 percent of their earned income, up to the FICA wage base. Taxpayers with less than $10,000 or $15,000 of earned income for single and joint returns, respectively, could exclude 20 percent of their total income up to $10,000 or $15,000.

[13] In B-G, deductions can only be used to calculate the tax subject to the 14 percent rate.

[14] B-G and R-M limit the exclusion of employer contributions to accident and health insurance to amounts attributable to providing wage replacement payments.

[15] Under D-S individuals would exclude fringe benefits, but businesses would not deduct compensation in the form of fringes.

[16] B-G and R-M would repeal exclusion but only to the extent that employer paid premiums exceed employee paid premiums.

[17] D-S would repeal charitable deduction for both businesses and individuals.

[18] B-G would limit the deduction to 50 percent of contributions.

[19] D-S would allow a deduction for business travel and entertainment expenses, if reasonable.

[20] B-G would tax estate and trusts at a 30% rate. K-K would tax estates and trusts at a 25% rate.

[21] D-S would reduce the incentive for income shifting by taxing all income at the 19 percent rate.

[22] D-S would provide dividend relief by taxing corporate income only once at the corporate level.

[23] For purposes of computing the base tax, B-G would retain the one-time exclusion of $125,000 of gain on the sale of a principal residence by taxpayers who are 55 years old or older. This exclusion would not apply for purposes of computing the surtaxes.

[24] K-K would reduce the capital gains tax rate to 20% for corporations. Capital losses would be deductible against ordinary income, but would be subject to the individual minimum tax. The one-time exclusion for $125,000 of gain on the sale of a principal residence by taxpayers who are 55 or older would be retained.

[25] R-M would repeal the one-time exclusion of gain from sale or exchange of principal residence.

[26] N-S would repeal the one time exclusion of $125,000 of gain on the sale of a principal residence for taxpayers 55 years old and older.

[27] R-M would allow individuals to expense certain equipment.

[28]R-M provides a new SUSA savings account with deductible annual limits of $10,000 ad $20,000 for single and joint returns, respectively. Funds could be used for non-retirement purposes. Income earned on the account would be tax-exempt until withdrawn.

[29]D-S would disallow the deduction for contributions to pension plans and would treat pension contributions as *compensation of the employee*.

[30]B-G would reduce limits on qualified pension plans from $30,000 *on defined contribution plans and* $90,000 *on defined benefit plans to* $15,000 and $45,000, respectively.

[31]D-S does not have a specific proposal on TFRP's, but would repeal all tax credits.

[32]B-G and K-K would repeal expensing of interest and taxes paid during the construction of a building and would require that these costs be amortized over 10 years.

[33]D-S would permit expensing of capital costs.

[34]B-G and K-K would repeal the deduction for bad debt reserves for financial institutions in excess of their actual experience.

[35]Under the business tax, interest paid to customers of financial institutions would not be deductible.

[36]For purposes of computing the base tax, B-G would allow itemized deductions for home mortgage interest and nonbusiness interest to the extent of investment income. For purposes of computing the surtaxes, investment interest is deductible to the extent of investment income.

[37]K-K would allow deductions for interest on loans to pay educational expenses, but not for other consumer debt.

[38]B-G would repeal deferral of foreign source income, DISC, and the exclusion of income of Americans working abroad. K-K would repeal DISC. R-M would repeal the exclusion of income of Americans working abroad. D-S would not tax the foreign source income of U.S. citizens and corporations, but would tax the U.S. source income of foreigners.

[39]N-S contains a special tax amnesty provision which waives the criminal and civil penalties for tax underpayment for taxpayers who agree to certain conditions.